THE MORMONS

OR LATTER-DAY SAINTS,

IN THE VALLEY OF THE GREAT SALT LAKE:

A HISTORY OF THEIR RISE AND PROGRESS,
PECULIAR DOCTRINES, PRESENT CONDITION,
AND PROSPECTS,
DERIVED FROM PERSONAL OBSERVATION,
DURING A RESIDENCE AMONG THEM

by

Lieut. John W. Gunnison

Reprint of the 1860 Lippincott Edition

Paradigm Publications — Brookline, Massachusetts

— 1993 —

Reprinted by

Paradigm Publications, Brookline Massachusetts

For information, inquire to Paradigm Publications, 44 Linden Street, Brookline Massachusetts 02146

Library of Congress Cataloging-in-Publication Data:

Gunnison, J. W. (John Williams), 1812-1853
The Mormons, or, Latter-day Saints, in the valley of the Great Salt Lake: their rise and progress, peculiar doctrines, present condition, and prospects, derived from personal observation, during a residence among them / by John W. Gunnison.
p. cm.

"Reprint of the 1860 Lippincott edition."
ISBN 0-912111-37-2 (cloth) : $20.00
1. Mormon Church--Utah--History--19th Century. 2. Church of Jesus Christ of Latter-Day Saints--Utah--History--19th century.
I. Title.
BX8611.G8 1992 92-25912
289.3'7924'09034--dc20 CIP
Rev

Editor's Preface

John Gunnison and the Mormons

This small volume is offered to contemporary readers as a memorial to its author, Captain John Williams Gunnison, of Goshen, New Hampshire, whose influence on Mormon and Western American History has been underestimated and neglected by historians. The 1860 edition also honors the memory of his wife, Martha Delony Gunnison, who persisted throughout her life in the belief that the Mormons were involved in the death of her husband. This fact is attested by her letter to Judge William W. Drummond and his response as published herein. The Gunnison Massacre, which also claimed the lives of artist Richard Kern, botanist Frederick Creutzfeldt, Mormon guide William Potter, employee John Bellows, and enlisted men Liptrot, Mertines, and Callfeldt, occurred near Sevier Lake, in Utah Territory, on October 26, 1853. This event was never investigated by competent authority during the lifetime of contemporaries. It has not been the subject of thorough historical research despite the fact that this massacre and its sequels were of pivotal importance in the history of Utah Territory.

Gunnison's book, at its appearance in 1852, had the distinction of being the first substantial and objective account of the Mormons after their westward movement, in 1847, from Illinois to the Great Basin of the Rocky Mountains. With remarkable brevity and accuracy, Gunnison devoted the first part of his book to a description of the beliefs and practices of the Mormon religion. He learned of them at first hand while serving as second in command with the Stansbury Expedition surveying the Great Salt Lake and Utah Lake in 1849-50. He gave unstinting praise to Mormon dedication and achievement in their hostile environment. He recognized their benefits to the nation as a supply point for westward emigration and acknowledged their positive influence on the Indian tribes among whom they settled.

While helping to prepare the official report of the Stansbury Expedition, Gunnison wrote the second part of his book, which related the origin and history of the Mormon movement according to his own investigation. His dedication to objectivity required that the rules of historical evidence be applied. The results were an unflattering description of the character and leadership of the Mormon Prophet, Joseph Smith; a view of the movement itself as an unfortunate delusion; and a belief that the Mormon persecutions were an inevitable though lamentable consequence of extravagant Mormon doctrines and practices which were greatly at variance with mainstream American values. These opinions soon attracted unfavorable reaction from Mormon readers.

Gunnison's final chapter was written at the height of a controversy which developed late in 1851, soon after the government of Utah Territory had begun to function. President Millard Fillmore had appointed the Mormon leader Brigham Young to be Governor of the Territory. Non-Mormons were appointed to the offices of Territorial Secretary and two of the three Federal Judgeships. The controversy involved prerogatives of office but soon spread to attitudes about unique Mormon beliefs and practices which the non-Mormon officers felt were either immoral or disloyal to the government. Believing their lives to be in danger, these "runaway" officials left the Territory.

Gunnison was in Washington at this time. He discounted the significance of the controversy and advised the President and other government officers to allow the Mormons to govern themselves with persons of their own choosing. He compared their demand for self-government to that of the American Colonies who rebelled against taxation without representation. Gunnison felt that the best policy was to "let them severely alone," using the expression the Mormons had adopted as policy toward the appointed officers they had rejected. His reasons for favoring the Mormons were not founded in his tolerance for the Mormon religion. Rather, he believed that Mormon unity had been achieved by persecution. If they were allowed to govern themselves in their isolated location, they could not claim to be persecuted. Under these conditions the internal weaknesses and inconsistencies of the religion would lead to division and remove any threat the Mormons might hold for the American Union. Gunnison's final chapter analyzes these weaknesses and is an eloquent expression of his belief in the power of freedom to shape institutional character.

Captain Gunnison was appointed to lead a survey expedition to explore a route for a railroad from Missouri to the Pacific Ocean in May, 1853. While in St. Louis, in June, he became aware of Mormon hostility toward his self-assumed role as a "chronicler" of their movement. Recognizing the need for Mormon support to the success of his expedition, Gunnison wrote letters to Brigham Young and to his Mormon associate in the earlier survey, Albert Carrington. He asked Carrington to begin survey operations between Salt Lake City and Fort Bridger and to provide guides and supplies for him upon his arrival in Utah Territory. He expressed his surprise that the Mormons were "down upon him" as an author.

At this same time, Mormon expansion of their settlements provoked conflict with the Utah Indians. The Mormons made preparations to defend themselves from this danger by cutting off all aid and trade with the Indians and by fortifying and "walling in" all of their towns and villages. This action, they believed, would also provide safety from thieves, from hostile emigrants and from military invasion, which they were taught to expect from the American nation and from other nations that would oppose the establishment of their Kingdom of God on earth.

The Mormon conflict with the Indians became most violent just as the Gunnison Expedition entered Utah Territory. Gunnison became aware of possible Indian danger to his own Expedition as he came to the village of Manti, on October 19, 1853. Despite the lack of communication from Governor Young or from Albert Carrington, Gunnison hired Mormon guides to help complete the survey. On the advice of these guides, he changed his earlier plan to follow the course of the Sevier River toward Sevier Lake. Instead, he went to Fillmore, the designated Mormon capital city, intending to approach Sevier Lake across Pahvant Valley.

While at Fillmore, Gunnison was told by village President Anson Call that local Indian conditions were dangerous. One of several nearby bands of Pahvantes, led by Chief Kanosh, had recently had a tragic encounter with a party of emigrants bound for California.

A band chief had been killed. Sons of the slain leader demanded vengeance. It is not certain Gunnison was told that the Indians had asked for Mormon help, or that when the Indians' own efforts at vengeance failed, the band threatened to attack Fillmore. When Brigham Young was informed of this danger, he sent his special Indian agent, Dimick Huntington, to Fillmore to appease the Indians. Captain Gunnison talked to Huntington, whom he knew from his earlier experience in Utah. He was assured that the problem had been solved. Peace had been guaranteed for the future in talks Huntington had held with Chief Kanosh and members of this band. This knowledge gave Gunnison "an unusual feeling of security," about this particular band of Indians.

Gunnison was anxious to complete his work near Sevier Lake so he could make a further survey up the Weber River to Fort Bridger and back by way of Timpanogos River. This was the task he had asked Carrington to perform prior to his arrival, but it had not been done. Cold weather had set in. Soon the mountain passes would be filled with snow, making further work toward Fort Bridger impossible until spring. Gunnison had to file his report before February. He wanted his superiors in Washington to know that there were excellent passages through the Rocky Mountains where a railroad could be built. This sense of urgency, together with his belief that the local Indians were friendly, led him to divide his survey party.

Upon reaching Gunnison Bend of the Sevier River near present Delta, the Captain led his party of twelve men down the river toward the lake. The balance of the expedition, under Lieutenant Edward G. Beckwith and Captain Robert M. Morris, turned east to explore the passage of the river through the mountains near present Leamington.

Gunnison's men were observed by the band of thirty Pahvant Indians who had threatened to "kill all Fillmore." They had not been contacted by Dimick Huntington and were still seeking vengeance for the death of their chief. The small group of Americans was a ready target for revenge as well as for their guns, ammunition, horses, gold and other booty. Under cover of darkness and dense vegetation, they surrounded the camp. Just at dawn they attacked the survey crew and soldiers with rifle fire and arrows. They killed Gunnison and seven others within a few minutes, then plundered and butchered their victims.

Four soldiers escaped. One made his way to Beckwith's camp and reported the massacre. Captain Morris with the remaining soldiers and the expedition's surgeon, set out to rescue possible survivors, meeting three other escaping soldiers enroute. They arrived near the scene, 28 miles distant, just at nightfall, where they discovered two dead and mutilated privates. Rather than risk ambush, the soldiers "stood to horse" through the night, while listening to the wolves devour their comrades.

At daybreak the soldiers advanced and found the mutilated bodies of the other victims. They were unable to bury the dead for they had brought no tools with them. In a vain effort, they broke their sabres in the frozen ground. They had to leave the bodies and return to protect the remainder of the survey party.

Lt. Beckwith and Capt. Morris wrote letters to their superiors reporting the massacre. These, and messages to Brigham Young, were delivered to Salt Lake City by Mormon couriers. Governor Young immediately dispatched Dimick Huntington to recover the government property and to retrieve and bury the remains of the dead, though these services were not requested by Beckwith and Morris. Huntington reported to Young the names of all persons involved in the massacre and all other details. This information was never made public.

In his official report of the massacre, Governor Young said Gunnison had been warned of Indian dangers but had used bad judgment by dividing his party and by his choice of an indefensible campsite. He said that the officers had quarreled among themselves and for this reason Gunnison's body was deliberately left unburied. He believed the Indians should not be "unduly censured" for their conduct and took no action to punish the guilty parties. In this and subsequent reports, Governor Young suppressed the fact of the threat to Fillmore, of Huntington's mission to resolve the conflict and of Huntington's bad advice to Gunnison.

Since no action had been taken by Territorial authority to punish the offending Indians or to seek justice through the courts, the War

Department ordered the Expedition of Lt. Col. Edward J. Steptoe, enroute to California in the summer of 1854, to stop over in Salt Lake City and take this necessary action. Colonel Steptoe acted on the advice of Governor Young to have the Indians deliver up the guilty parties rather than to capture and punish the entire band, which the Colonel had intended to do.

In the spring of 1855, Chief Kanosh surrendered six Indians of the band which had killed the Gunnison party. This number, the chief said, would "equalize the balance of killing." Only three of those surrendered were warriors. These were indicted by a grand jury, then tried and found guilty. The jury rendered a verdict of manslaughter despite specific instruction from the Judge that this was proved to be a case of premeditated murder. Nevertheless, the verdict was accepted and the prisoners were sentenced to three years in jail.

Colonel Steptoe, the Judge, and the prosecuting attorneys, were incensed by what they believed to be a miscarriage of justice. They wrote angry letters to the several Federal agencies they represented, charging the Mormons with defiance of law and failure to discharge their obligations as citizens. It was claimed they did this in obedience to orders covertly given from Brigham Young. A report of the trial, prefaced with acrimonious charges against the Mormons, was sent to the *New York Times.* Another copy was sent to the *San Francisco Daily Herald,* adding the fact that the prisoners had been allowed to escape.

This angry encounter was made worse by complicating circumstances. While in Utah, Colonel Steptoe was appointed by President Franklin Pierce to succeed Brigham Young as Territorial Governor. The appointment required that Steptoe resign his military commission. Steptoe was willing to accept the appointment provided he could resume his military rank upon completion of his duties as governor. This matter was not resolved before he left the Territory in the spring of 1855.

Another complication was created by the involvement of soldiers and Mormon women through the winter. When the soldiers left for California in the spring, nearly 100 Mormon women, anxious to escape polygamy, left with them. To inform the public of the Mormon side of this confrontation, Brigham Young had many affidavits created, charging the soldiers and non-Mormon public officials with drunkenness, gambling, sexual abuses and other irregularities. These were sent to the War Department in Washington as evidence of renewed persecution of the Mormons. These charges and counter charges greatly antagonized public opinion against the Mormons, producing results contrary to what Captain Gunnison had hoped for.

A further conflict arising from the Gunnison Massacre occurred following the appointment of William W. Drummond, of Illinois, as a Federal Judge for Utah Territory. Upon assuming his duties in 1855, Judge Drummond declared the Mormon Probate Courts to be illegal, creating great antagonism against himself. His personal character and his cohabitation with a known harlot, passed off as his wife, also offended the Mormons, particularly because of their polygamous marriage practices. At Fillmore, as related in his letter to Mrs. Gunnison, herein, Judge Drummond tried several cases related to the Gunnison Massacre. He became convinced that the Mormons were the perpetrators of, and perhaps participants in the massacre. His antagonism against the Mormons was heightened by ostracism, as the policy of leaving him "severely alone" was applied through the winter of 1855-56.

During Judge Drummond's tenure, Brigham Young launched extensive programs to occupy territory open to his control and to gain influence in the American nation. He created the Deseret Express and Carrying Company to establish freight and mail relay stations from Missouri to San Francisco. He devised the inexpensive handcart method of bringing thousands of converts from Europe to Western America, intending to establish villages along the emigration route and to populate additional territories in the American Union. He also undertook a comprehensive religious reformation to purify his people so they could exercise the power of God to aid in the completion of their divine mission. These efforts increased internal dissent, particularly when the handcart expedition proved disastrous. The heightened religious zeal produced violence against dissenting Mormons and Federal officers not of the Mormon faith. In the spring of 1857, most of the non-Mormon Federal officers and many discontented Mormons left the Territory bearing tales of Mormon misdeeds. These reports increased public reaction against the Mormons.

Matters came to a climax beginning with the election of James Buchanan as President, in 1856. Americans were greatly concerned with slavery in Kansas and with polygamy in Utah, as well as with evidences of violence and disloyalty in both territories. The emerging Republican political party sought to capitalize on these concerns by advocating Federal control of territorial development. The Dred Scott decision in March, 1857, which favored slave-holding interests, further undermined the moderate Democratic platform upon which Buchanan had been elected. His party was pressed to prove they could control anarchy in the developing territories. President Buchanan assigned General W. S. Harney to command a military force to aid the Territorial government in Kansas. He replaced Brigham Young as Governor and ordered an army under the command of Colonel Albert S. Johnston to accompany the new Governor to aid in the enforcement of the law, if necessary, in Utah Territory.

Buchanan's intended actions toward Utah Territory were confirmed to be necessary by further excitement created at that moment by Judge Drummond. The Judge had been absent from his post in Utah for almost a year by the time President Buchanan decided to take action. During this time, Drummond was in California where he wrote newspaper articles denouncing Mormon behavior, using the pen names Amicus Curiae and Verastus. In April, 1857, the Judge traveled east by way of Panama to New Orleans, where he wrote a letter of resignation to the Justice Department. Drummond gave as his reason for resigning, the ungovernable nature of the Mormons under the leadership of Brigham Young. He cited many cases of unlawful conduct, including murderous assaults against dissenters and involvement of Mormons in the massacre of Captain Gunnison and his men. These accusations were read by Captain Gunnison's widow, who wrote to the Judge that she also believed the Mormons were involved in the death of her husband. These charges received great publicity during April and May, 1857. The Mormons responded by attacking the moral character of Judge Drummond.

Brigham Young learned of his replacement and of the troops ordered to Utah from newspaper accounts. At first he was willing to step aside, but he changed his mind. He decided to treat the American army as a mob and took actions to prevent their entry into the

Territory. He declared martial law, activated the Militia and enlisted the active support of Indian bands throughout the Territory, intending to wage war if necessary. The impending conflict was foretold in the brutal assassination of Mormon Apostle Parley Pratt, in Arkansas, by the husband of one of Pratt's plural wives. In the intensity of these circumstances, during the month of September, a party of more than one hundred emigrants from Arkansas, Missouri, and Illinois, traveling through Utah Territory, were attacked at Mountain Meadow and brutally massacred by Indians and Mormons.

Mormon resistance against the army evoked public sympathy for their defense of religious freedom. But the deceit and vengeance exhibited in the Massacre at Mountain Meadow, when revealed, finally destroyed all favorable impressions. These negative views henceforth dominated American opinion about the Mormons. An era ended as the American army occupied Utah Territory and Brigham Young was replaced as Governor. It was under these conditions that the 1860 edition of Gunnison's book was issued, adding the letters of Mrs. Gunnison and Judge Drummond as they appear in this reprint.

Captain Gunnison's book, the Gunnison Massacre, and its several sequels had much to do with the course and outcome of the Mormon movement during these early years. The charges of Mormon involvement in that affair by Mrs. Gunnison and Judge Drummond, among others, were neglected due to the more compelling need to deal with Brigham Young's resistance to the army and then with the horrible Massacre at Mountain Meadow. Soon the Civil War intervened. For thirty years afterward, the Mormons were under the pressure of Federal law to abandon polygamy and the political aspects of theocracy in order to attain self-government as a state in the Union. These more demanding issues left the Gunnison Massacre as unfinished business. It is to that task, as well as to an assessment of the role of John W. Gunnison in his service to the nation, that this reprint of his book is dedicated.

Robert Kent Fielding
Dorothy Stratton Fielding
Brookline, Massachusetts, 1993

Portrait of John Williams Gunnison.
From Nolie Mumey, **John Williams Gunnison.**

NAUVOO

THE MORMONS,

OR,

LATTER-DAY SAINTS,

IN THE VALLEY OF

The Great Salt Lake:

A HISTORY OF

THEIR RISE AND PROGRESS, PECULIAR DOCTRINES, PRESENT CONDITION, AND PROSPECTS,

DERIVED FROM

PERSONAL OBSERVATION;

DURING A RESIDENCE AMONG THEM.

By Lieut. J. W. GUNNISON,

OF THE TOPOGRAPHICAL ENGINEERS

PHILADELPHIA:
J. B. LIPPINCOTT & CO.
1860.

TO THE

COMMANDING OFFICER

OF THE

EXPLORING EXPEDITION TO THE GREAT SALT LAKE OF UTAH,

CAPT. HOWARD STANSBURY, T. E.,

WHO HAS SO ABLY GIVEN THE OFFICIAL AND SCIENTIFIC RESULTS OF THE

SURVEYS IN THE COUNTRY OF

"THE LATTER-DAY SAINTS,"

TO WHICH THIS BOOK APPENDS THEIR

HISTORY AND THEOLOGY,

AND IN PLEASANT RECOLLECTION OF OUR TOUR IN THE ROCKY MOUNTAINS,

IS THIS RESPECTFULLY

DEDICATED.

PREFACE.

THIS treatise on the faith and condition of the Mormons, results from a careful observation of that strange and interesting people, during more than a year's residence among them, in an official capacity. It was conceived, that what is influencing the conscientious character of a half million souls, is worthy a serious investigation, though not pertinent to official report under government auspices.

No apology for error is here set forth, though the persecution of its advocates is deprecated.

The writer has undertaken neither the task of criticism nor controversy. His aim is not "to shoot folly as it flies," but to let folly tire on its own pinions, and reason regain its sway over erratic feeling, when the mists of prejudice on one side, and of fanaticism on the other, are dispelled by the light of knowledge.

For those who desire *facts* in the history of humanity, on which to indulge in reflection, is this offered. It were far easier to give a romantic sketch in lofty metaphors, of the genesis and exodus of the empire-founding Saints — the subject is its own epic of heroism, whose embellishment is left to imaginative genius, and its philosophy to be deduced by the candid philanthropist.

Truth and justice, in few words, and as near as possible to fallible human observation, is what this exposition aims at. Facts of motive and history are collected, which concern a portion of our own fellow-citizens. These are the scholars of the workshop and the field—the leaders are students of men and things. They have been schooled in patience, perseverance, and self-denial—men of action, tried in varied circumstances.

My thanks are due to my friend F. R. Grist, Esq., for the view of the "theo-democràtic" capital of Deserét. That gentleman accompanied the expedition thither, and, as an amateur, freely gave illustrations of the romantic scenery, for the public report printed by the United States Senate. What is there fully portrayed, is here lightly touched, for the Mormons constitute the picture attempted to be given, and other circumstances the frame in which it is set.

JULY, 1852.

NARRATIVE

OF THE

DEATH OF CAPT. GUNNISON.

THE subjoined letter from Judge Drummond to Mrs. M. D. Gunnison contains the most authentic account of the death of the lamented author of this volume, and his party, in Utah, in 1853. The stoutest heart will recoil with horror from this recital of the most brutal outrage ever committed on Western territory, and every American will regret that a full measure of justice has not been dealt out to the fiendish perpetrators of this cold-blooded murder: —

BETHLEHEM, PA., *April* 14, 1857.

JUDGE DRUMMOND: —

You will please recognise in me the widow of Capt. Gunnison. I have just finished your letter of resignation to the Attorney General, and see confirmed by you the impression I have always held myself, that the Mormons were the directors of my husband's murder, notwithstanding I have, both from Brigham Young and Carrington, received the kindest letters of condolence, &c. Pardon me, then, my dear sir, for thus intruding myself upon you; but if you can find the leisure, you will confer a lasting favor upon us by giving us the particulars of such information as you have gleaned. You can better imagine, than I can by words express, the feelings that thus influence me to impose this much upon your time.

M. D. Gunnison.

Chicago, Ill., *April* 27, 1857.

Mrs. M. D. Gunnison, *Bethlehem, Pa.*

My Dear Strange Friend: — Your kind note of inquiry, under date of the 14th inst., was duly received at this place on the 21st inst., but owing to personal matters, I have been wholly unable to reply to your letter until this day, for which delay I trust your generous heart will find no fault. You ask me "to give the particulars of such information as I have gleaned" in connection with the murder of Capt. John W. Gunnison, who was most foully and inhumanly murdered on the Sevier river, in Utah Territory, in A. D. 1853. This information I will cheerfully give you, not only as a sense of duty to you as the wife of a good man, who fell prematurely at his post doing duty, but as a matter of fact, which should go to the world as a portion of the history of that barbarous transaction.

In the month of November, A. D. 1853, Captain Gunnison and eight others (one of whom was a Mormon), were murdered on the Sevier river, in Utah Territory, and the report was quite current that they were murdered by the Indians; subsequently, at a session of the Grand Jury in Juab county, Utah Territory, Hon. John F. Kinney, presiding, twenty-six Indians of the Parvante tribe were indicted for the said murder, and, by some arrangement between Col. E. J. Steptoe, of the United States Army, and Kanash, the Chief of the Parvante tribe, eight Indians (some of whom were squaws, and one old blind Indian man,) were put upon their trial for murder, at Nephi City; and, strange to say, a Mormon jury found the Indian warriors not guilty, and as against the old, crippled, and measureably blind Indians, three in number, found a verdict of manslaughter, and they were sentenced to three years imprisonment in the penitentiary of Utah, being the full length of time prescribed by the statute for such offences. These verdicts, and the finding of the juries under the law and the evidence, so wounded and mortified Judge Kinney, that he at once adjourned the court, unavoidably coming to the conclusion that there was false dealing somewhere; and in fact, not only he, but Col. Steptoe, Gen. Holman, the Government Attorney, Hon. Garland Hurt, the Indian Agent of the Territory, Capt. James B. Leach, the mail contractor between San Diego in California and Salt Lake City, and Columbus L. Craig, all of whom were cognizant of the influences brought to bear on the trial, arrived irresistibly at the conclusion that the Indians were found not guilty by order of the church, and that Dimick B. Huntington, an Indian interpreter, and spiritual brother-in-law of Gov. Brigham Young, was the man who bore the decree and order of the church to the jury, who implicitly found the verdicts according to the mandates of the church, as is now the universal rule and order of jury trials "in the peaceful valleys of the mountains."

At the November term of my court, held at Fillmore City, in the year 1855, one Levi Abrams, a Jewish Mormon, was put upon his trial for the wilful and unprovoked murder of Toebe, a favorite warrior of the Parvante band, and during that trial much was said by both Indian and white witnesses relative to the murder of Captain Gunnison and his party, which raised strong presumptions in my mind that certain white men were *particeps criminis* to that cruel murder, but not wholly conclusive. In this case the jury, true to the law of the church, and basely false to the law of the land, found Abrams not guilty.

At the same court, a favorite Indian warrior of Gov. Young, by the name of Eneis, was put upon his trial for the murder of Captain Gunnison and others, to which I particularly allude in this letter and at this time, and, upon his trial I became convinced beyond the possibility of a doubt, that the whole affair was a deep and maturely laid plan to murder the whole party of engineers, or surveyors, and charge the murders upon the Indians (who, by the way, have the credit for killing a great many persons). In the trial of the warrior Eneis, the evidence disclosed the fact that he was the property of Governor Young, and that he could speak English quite fluently, and that, when he left the city of Salt Lake, he went under the order of Governor Young and the church. Again, it was repeatedly proven that Eneis was in company with several white men on the day before the murder, and that they were all on their way toward the engineers' camp.

Again, it was proven on the same trial by a number of Indian witnesses, that only four shots were fired by the Indians, and that all the rest were fired by the Mormons, and that, by order and direction of the Mormons, the Indians sprang out of the ambush, where they lay disguised during the night before the firing, which occurred about sunrise in the morning, and went across the river to scalp and otherwise maltreat the men in their agonies of death, but more particularly to save the Mormon who fell in the fight, provided he was not fatally wounded, and told the Indians how they could recognise the Mormon from the Americans, which was by certain peculiar marks on the garment which he wore next his body; but the poor fellow, with the other eight, had received a fatal shot, and died on the ground with his priestly robe worn next to his body. The white men were so accurately described, that any one acquainted with the principal men of the Mormon church could quite readily select the men as described by Old Pareshont and Heap of Elk, as well as several others equally as honest and intelligent, who were the principal witnesses in behalf of the Government. And right here I have no hesitation in saying who some of them are and were, and this I do for the benefit of those men who may go to Utah as appointees under the present administration, viz.: William A. Hickman, Anson Call, Alexander McRay, Ephraim Hanks, James W. Cummings, Edwin D. Wolley, George Peacock, Levi Abrams, and —— Bronson, all of whom are in good fellowship and standing to this day in the church; and although the evidence on behalf of the Government against Eneis was clear and conclusive, and no rebutting evidence, the Mormon jury, true to the order of the holy priesthood, found a verdict of not guilty.

And here, my dear friend, painful and revolting as it is, the true history of that sad scene requires me to say that the evidence disclosed the fact that several Indian warriors crossed the Sevier river immediately after seeing that they had accomplished the work for which they were set apart, and proceeded to cut off the legs and arms of the men while in the agonies of death;

also, to scalp them, and then rifle their pockets of their contents; and take off their clothes and put them on themselves; and that Eneis, the then prisoner at the bar, cut Capt. Gunnison's body open and took out his heart while he was yet alive, and the heart so full of blood that it bounded on the ground after being taken out; and not content with this, but cut out his tongue, and otherwise cut and mangled his body.

True it is, my dear friend, I know that this dark and bloody picture will prostrate every nerve of your tender form; and painful and heart-sickening as it is for me to think of, let alone pen anything in connection with that revolting murder, but duty to you, duty to the country, duty to a broken and violated law, duty to bleeding and down-trodden humanity, duty to a correct history in connection with the dark and bloody code of the order of the High Priesthood of the Utah Mormons, and above all, duty to the fair reputation of a brother officer engaged in the faithful discharge of his duty, and one who fell in the noonday of life at the hands of an organized band of systematic pirates, robbers, and murderers, and whose blood yet cries to heaven for a witness to attest in thunder-tones the dread but sad and solemn truth connected with his tragic fate, all seem to require that when I answer his wife, the companion of his youth, who so naturally applies to the man, of all others, possessed of the legal truths con-

2

nected with this history, and I should tell them precisely as they are, and not suppress any part thereof.

I can well imagine, Madam, your long sufferings and anxieties relative to the death of your husband, and I most truly assure you that your conclusions relative to his death were well founded. I leave you and all others to conclude whether I am not fully justified in my conviction in the premises, and whether I could have rationally come to any other conclusion than the one to which I here refer, as well as in my letter of resignation to Attorney-General Black.

With an ardent desire that you may live to a ripe old age, enjoy all the blessings which this life can afford, and, above all, in that list of blessings, good health, live to see the day when the foul stain of Mormon oppression and tyranny shall be effectually checked in this our happy country, your husband's untimely death vindicated by the courts and laws of this land, and, after death, in that Grand Lodge above be re-united to the partner and companion of your youth.

W. W. Drummond.

CONTENTS.

PART I.

CHAPTER VI.

CHAPTER VII.

PART II.

RISE AND EARLY PROGRESS OF MORMONISM.

CHAPTER I.

CHAPTER II.

CHAPTER III.

CHAPTER IV.

CHAPTER V.

CHAPTER VI.

CHAPTER VII.

CHAPTER VIII.

HISTORY

OF

THE MORMONS.

DOMESTIC POLICY OF THE MORMONS.

CHAPTER I.

THEIR COUNTRY.

AMONG the teeming events of the present era, one of the most remarkable is the formation of a state by a peculiar people, in the far interior of America, which has assumed the name of Des-er-ét,—a mystic word, taken from the Book of Mormon,* signifying, the Land of the Honey-Bee.

Its present capital and principal settlement is in the valley of the Great Salt Lake. In this and contiguous vales are the gardens of the mountains, in which the bee and its fostering companion, man, have lately been colonized, and from which neither will carry away the stores gathered into the domestic hive. Industrious alike, the sweet bounties of Providence are collected,

* The "Latter-Day Saint pretend to derive the word Mormon from the Gaelic and a branch of the Teutonic dialects: compounding it from Mor, *more* or *great*, and from Mon, signifying *good*, and therefore it imports—more good, great good. Mormon, mormonos, Greek, signifies a female spectre, a phantom, a hideous monster.

These two definitions may be deemed to convey the different opinions of the supporters and opposers of Mormonism.

to be luxuriated upon at home, in all the freedom of their being and constitution of their nature. This valley is situated midway between the states of the great Mississippi and the golden empire rising to life and influence on the shores of the Pacific Ocean. It is isolated from habitable grounds; having inhospitable tracts to the north and south, and the untimbered slope of the Rocky Mountains, nearly a thousand miles wide, on the east, and nearly a thousand miles of arid salt-deserts on the west, broken up by frequent ridges of sterile mountains. This fertile tract, therefore, presents itself to us with varied associations, an object of curious contemplation.

The Mormon settlements are in that remarkable depression styled The Great Basin—a region embraced in the Rocky Mountain land out of which no waters flow. That Alpine district extends along the western side of the American continent, covering sixteen degrees of longitude in the Utah latitudes, and is a succession of nearly parallel mountain ranges, having a north and south direction. Between these ridges are the valleys, whose average width may be twenty miles. In some places, the ranges are abruptly terminated for a space, leaving a gap, termed a kanyon, or pass, according to the width of the break in the mountain. These are names given by the trappers, who were the pioneer white men into those solitudes.

The absence of one or more short ranges, opposite each other, will occasionally unite several valleys into one. It is through the kanyons or narrow gorges, with perpendicular sides of rock, and the still wider passes into the plains between, that remarkably level routes for travel are found across the continent. The "South Pass" in the great eastern chain, is more than a hundred miles long, or wide, as it is usual to designate it, and then going west, you enter the great coal basin through which Green river flows. A narrower pass is near Bear river, and crossing over a gentle swell, one enters the Weber river kanyon, and emerging upon the beautiful Kamas prairie, that extends to the Timpanogas, the road lies down its bank into Utah valley. Here the choice of northern or southern routes is offered. The one by the Mary's river is most followed in summer; but a high pass on the Sierra Nevada has to be surmounted. The other is south-westerly in direction, across the Great Basin, and doubles the mountain into the head of the Tulare valleys, whence the way to San Francisco, or some Pacific port, is to be selected on feasible and fertile ground.

The Great Basin is that high level, over four thousand feet above the ocean, between the Nevada and Wahsatch ranges. It is a desert in character, with some fertile strips flanking the bases of the highest ridges. This vast region is mountainous; the ranges generally from two to three thousand feet high, and parallel with the main ones on the sides, with some partial cross ridges that form minor basins. In the interior, therefore, fresh water becomes scarce, for these hills do not collect sufficient snow in winter, the only wet season, to furnish irrigating streams, and fertilize the bench of alluvion at their base, or water the plains between; and the consequence follows that these tracts are parched and arid, and frequently so impregnated with alkali as to make them unfit for vegetable life. Artemisias and Salicornias contend for a miserable existence on portions of the plains; and bunch grass furnishes grazing on the hill-sides for antelope and deer. There is not properly a "rim," or continuous mountain, particularly on the north; but a "divide" between the parallel ranges, which is sometimes a swamp, out of which the waters flow in contrary directions; and the position of this feature may be observed, on the map of the Great Valley, to the west of Bear river. This interior basin is about five hundred miles in diameter either way, and in the eastern part have the Mormons settled.

Along the western foot of the Wahsatch range, for three hundred miles, is a strip of alluvion, from one to two miles in width,—and, in the valley of the Jordan, this is widened by what can be reclaimed by irrigating from its waters; and the spots similarly situated, in other valleys, furnish the only land suited to cultivation in the Utah Territory. This arises from the want of rain during the growing season; and water for the crops is only to be procured from the numerous streams that flow down the mountain gorges, fed during the spring, and into midsummer, by the melting snows. The higher mountains retain the snow, and irrigate the bases the longest time, and where the streams cannot be taken at the kanyon mouths, and led off for the farmer's use, the ground is lost to the plough. Most of these creeks are absorbed in the porous alluvion before they have reached a mile from the base, and frequently re-appear in very diminished quantity in springs, at too low a level for use, in the arid plain that borders the salt pools or lakes. The land around Salt Lake is flat, and rises imperceptibly on the south and west for several miles, where it is not broken up by the abrupt hills, and is a soft and sandy barren, irreclaimable for agricultural purposes. On the north the tract is narrow, and the springs bursting out near the surface of the water, the grounds cannot be irrigated; but the eastern side, above the line of overflow when the lake rises with the spring freshets, is fertile and cultivated between the mountain and shore.

On the south of the lake, and above the alkaline barrens, lie the more fertile valleys of the Jordan and Tuilla, separated by the Oquirrh Mountain; and these are divided from the plains which lie to the south, between the same ranges, by the Traverse Mountain, which is a cross ridge, diminishing in height to the westward. Here is fine grazing during the entire year, and the east of Jordan Valley is watered by bold streams that traverse a strip of alluvion twenty miles long by eight in width, to the banks of the Jordan. This great stream rushes with a foaming torrent through the kanyon cut in the cross range, and descends about one hundred feet in a distance of two miles, where the current becomes more gentle and winding, to the great lake below. The banks are steep and high, immediately below the kanyon, but gradually retreat and slope away to the Oquirrh hills, and a canal can easily be carried on the level of the kanyon, winding on a curve to Spring Point, twenty miles from the city. The chalky waters of the Jordan can be used for irrigating eighty additional square miles in the valley, and furnish water-power very accessible, and to any required extent, for milling, machinery, or manufactures. Ascending the Traverse range, a beautiful panorama of lake, plain, and river, embosomed with lofty and romantic mountains, bursts upon the view. Here is the lovely Utah Lake and its winding outlet; and the Timpanogas, with four other rivers, fringed with cottonwoods, a sight so seldom seen in these regions, and, by contrast, enchanting. All the valley on the east side of the lake is fertile, and the waters throughout fresh and sparkling, as they rapidly descend to the quiet reservoir.

The valleys afford perennial pasturage, but the hill-sides furnish the bunch grass only during the warm months of the year. It seeds in summer, and is germinated by the autumnal rains, and grows under the snowy covering of winter. In the spring, as the snow-line retreats up the slope, under the melting influence of the approaching sun, the cattle and wild grazing animals follow it to the mountain peaks until midsummer, to be driven down again as the accumulating snow, beginning on the summits about the equinox, descends in a few weeks to the base. When it rains on the valleys, the snow falls on the mountains, and, during winter, an immense quantity is drifted into the kanyons and passes, to the depth sometimes of hundreds of feet, blocking up the roads, and making prisoners at home, those who sojourn in those solitudes.

The difficulty in procuring fencing materials, has caused the fields to be left imperfectly enclosed, and slightly protected; and it becomes necessary to set the youth to attend the cattle during the day, and drive them to the *corrals*, or fenced yards, at night. This position of these two descriptions of land, the cultivated and the waste, renders the people there residing, equally a pastoral and an agricultural community. All the cultivated lands, that is, those brought under irrigation, can be allotted to raising cereals and vegetables. The flocks and herds driven to the hills in summer, and fed upon the plains in winter, will furnish one half the provisions required to sustain the population that can be accommodated on the cultivated belt between the pastures. The soil, in its mineral composition, is of the most fertile description, having been formed out of disintegrated feldspathic rocks of the summits, and mixed with the debris and decomposed limestones from the lower altitudes. As many as sixty bushels of wheat are usually grown to the acre, and when strict regard has been paid to watering the crops, a greater yield has been given, and, in one instance, a hundred and eighty fold was reaped from the drilling of one bushel upon three acres; and the average of sustenance from root crops is more abundant still. The potato grows luxuriantly, and of a delightful quality, and the sugar-beet attains to an enormous size, from which good molasses is manufactured; and the attempt will soon be made to extract sugar from the same, to supply the demands of the market.

In order to estimate the probable amount of population which can well be sustained in the territory, we may safely rely on an equivalent of two thousand pounds of flour to the acre of the plowed lands, and, drawing the meat part of the ration, or one half, from the herds fed elsewhere, there could be fed four thousand persons on the square mile. Such a density of inhabitants it can hardly be supposed will ever be attained there; but, modified by the peculiar circumstances of the case, and social character of the people, and giving a far less amount to the mile, we may calculate that the territory of Utah will maintain, with ease, a million of inhabitants. Stretching southward from the point we have been noticing, and passing over the rim of the Great Basin into a cotton-growing region, and where it is contemplated to try the sugar-cane; having abundant iron mines every where in its whole extent, and inexhaustible beds of coal in the Green River Basin—with hill pastures, the finest in the world for sheep and wool raising—with water-power for manufactures on every considerable stream—there are elements for a great and powerful mountain nation; and the part such a force could play toward those on either side is not an insignificant one for our consideration.

There are three salt lakes in Central Utah; the greatest of them surrounded with romantic scenery, and invested with interest by many a legend among the early discoverers and mountain trappers. The water is perfectly saturated with salt, and so dense that persons float, corklike, on its waves, or stand suspended with ease, with the shoulders exposed above the surface.

The shores of its bays in summer are lined with the skeletons and larvæ of insects, and the few fish that venture too far from the mouths of the rivers; and these form banks that fester and ferment, emitting sulphurous gases, offensive to the smell, but not supposed deleterious to health; and these, often dispersed by storms, are at last thrown far up the beach to dry into hard cakes of various dimensions, on which horses can travel without breaking them through; the underside being moist, the masses are slippery and insecure. The salt-boilers affirm that they obtain two measures of salt from three of the brine, and they have christened this sheet of water, which is seventy miles long, with the name of the "Great Briny Shallow." There are several beautiful islands enclosed, two of them of considerable magnitude, with a mountain ridge through the centre two thousand feet high, and fresh springs of water, which have caused them to be selected by the shepherds and herdsmen for their occupation. The silence that surrounds one when standing on these islands, and having an unobstructed view of every part of the vast expanse, is very impressive; and as he floats on the surface of the waves, the eye traces several terraces around the contour of the islands, and along the adjacent mountains, on the whole circumference parallel with the horizon; and they seem to indicate that these have once been the borders of a mighty inland sea, whose waters retired suddenly to certain distances, by regular upheavings of the land, or equal outbreaks, to a lower level. Three principal terraces, each retreating about fifty feet above the other, may be counted; and their exact planes and magnitude show the comparison of the works of nature with the feeble imitations of man, in beauty, sublimity, and permanence.

At the base of the hills, around the lake, issue numerous warm springs, that collect in pools and smaller lakes; inviting aquatic fowl, during the winter, to resort to their agreeable temperature, and where insect larva furnishes food at all times; and the soil is so heated that snow cannot lie in their vicinity. In some places springs of different temperatures are in close proximity, some so hot that the hand cannot be thrust into them without pain; and near the Bear is a depression, in which issue three fountains between the strata, within a space of thirty feet; of which one is a hot sulphur, the next tepid and salt, and the uppermost, cool, delicious drinking water—the three currents unite, and flow off through the plain, a large and bold river. There are also warm "breathing" or gas-intermitting fountains, chalybeate and gypsum springs, of high and low temperatures. Those in the vicinity of the city have been arranged into delightful bathing reservoirs and bath-houses, out of the tithing fund, to which all are counselled to resort for cleanliness and health, at so small a charge, that it becomes a public luxury, safe and beneficial. It is a refreshing and delightful sport to bathe in the Salt Lake, but on emerging, the person is completely frosted over in purest white, and a fresh spring is a necessary appendage—it may be called the whitewashing ewer, applicable to the body if not the character.

Wild game abounds for the table, in the antelope, deer, and feathered tribes—the bear, panther, and smaller animals of prey, for the adventurous sportsman, range through hill, valley, and desert; and the angler can choose his fish, either in the swift torrents of the kanyons, where the trout delights to live, or in the calmer currents on the plains, where he will find abundance of the pike, the perch, the bass, and the chub. Along the brackish streams, from the saline springs, grows a thick tangled grass, and the marshy flats are covered with fine reeds or dense festucas. In early summer the shepherd lads fill their baskets with the eggs deposited in that cover by the goose, the duck, the curlew, and plover; or, taking a skiff, they can row to the Salt Lake islands, and freight to the water's edge with those layed for successive broods by the gull, the pelican, the blue heron, the crane, and the brandt.

Every day of the year has a different landscape for the eye, in the variety of light and shade cast by the sun, as he approaches toward, and recedes from, those frowning cliffs and snow-clad peaks — and the different coloured garb of the seasons, *nature's* change of fashions, so much imitated by the lovers of dress, on whom her lessons are not bestowed in vain, comes to aid in breaking up the monotony. On the south-east rises the lofty head of the Lone Peak, with double buttressed pillars on the summit, that look like an open portal to giant chambers in the clouds; and not far off, on the north, stand the Twin Peaks, side by side, like conjugal partners hesitating awhile on earth, before they pass through this inviting door to mansions amid the stars. When these barren masses of grey rock are viewed near at hand, the mind labors under its load of sublimity, grandeur, and awe—but when standing on some distant eminence, the eye seems to grasp the infinite before it, and distance softens the harsh outlines into wavy curves, with closing vistas between, lost in the horizon's edge; the senses become enraptured for awhile with vastness and beauty combined; but soon there comes welling up from the depths of the soul the feeling that something still is wanting, and coldness, sterility, and vacuity broods over the landscape. The full charm is not there—for the accessories of art spring not forth to make an agreeable variety, nor the forest-trees pointing to the skies, under whose shady retreats the weary of earth may contemplate their destiny.

Hidden away in the profound chasms and along the streams whose beds are deeply worn in the mountain sides are the cedar, pine dwarf-maple, and occasionally oak, where the inhabitants of the vale seek their fuel and building-timber, making journeys to obtain these necessaries from twenty to forty miles from their abodes.

The more exposed parts of the country are annually run over by the fires set by the Indians to kill and roast the crickets which they gather in summer for winter food. These fires ascend the furzy hill-sides and penetrate the forest kanyons—and it is a beautiful but melancholy sight to see the withered vegetation swept away by the curling flames as they leap up the cliffs, lighting up at night the surrounding country with fitful splendours. One of the strenuous efforts making to improve the country, is to arrest this destructive process and convert the prairies into desirable woodlands

The atmosphere of the valley is light, and breathing is a real luxury. The view being so unobstructed, an idea is prevalent that small objects can be seen at great distances distinctly, and some have asserted that a man could be noticed at fifty or a hundred miles. This is erroneous. In winter, if snow covers the ground, and the cold air is free from moisture, a dark object shows very far: — but in summer the atmosphere is filled with clouds of floating insects that give a bluish haze, and make it a labor for the eye to use telescopes for geodetic purposes, and astronomical observations on the sun are very imperfect. On the barren plains and the arid valleys, after the dry season has a little advanced, the mirage will take up objects and distort them in the most fantastic manner; treos, rocks like houses, artemisia patches, and the white alkaline efflorescing flats, will seem to vibrate and pass before you like a panorama of garden groves, with beautiful parterres and pleasure-loving lakes and castellated mansions: — a small stick close at hand will start up an immense giant at a distance; and far off things mock you with their retreatings as you endeavor to reach them; thinking that a few minutes may bring you to the landmarks or a pool of fresh water; and when hours of weary travel have elapsed, your disappointment is complete as they sink out of sight beneath the horizon above which refraction has raised them. Sometimes a man walking alone, will be multiplied into a troop marching with beautiful military exactness, and a few horsemen riding in a disorderly manner converted into a troop performing various evolutions; and where then is reason to apprehend that enemies are near, there imagination lends a fearful aid to magnify the picture, and you must be careful to take the description of a mountain guide with its due share of exaggeration.

At the mouth of the kanyons the breezes at night are ever fresh and strong: they issue into the valley and are occasioned by descending currents of air, cooled on the higher peaks and summits behind, and blow like the stream from a funnel; which makes the residence near those openings in summer a safe retreat from the attacks of the universal mosquito, and the "sand flies" or "brulés" that in unprotected places annoy the denizens.

CHAPTER II.

CIVIL AND THEOCRATICAL CHARACTER.

SUCH then is the general appearance of the country settled by the Mormons, and for a minute description, I beg leave to refer to the able report of the Surveying Expedition by Capt. H. Stansbury laid before Congress. But the peculiar character of the founders of Deserét, their energy, union and hopes, stimulated by their religious views, more especially demand our notice; and this subject is equally interesting to the politician, the philosopher, and the theologian. We found them, in 1849, organized into a state with all the order of legislative, judicial, and executive offices regularly filled, under a constitution eminently republican in sentiment, and tolerant in religion; and though the authority of Congress has not yet sanctioned this form of government, presented and petitioned for, they proceed quietly with all the routine of an organized self-governing people, under the title of a Territory; — being satisfied to abide their time, in accession of strength by numbers, when they may be deemed fit to take a sovereign position; being contented so long as allowed to enjoy the substance, under the shadow of a name. They lay and collect taxes, raise and equip troops for protection, in full sovereignty, on the soil they helped to conquer first, and subdue to use afterward.

While professing a complete divorce of church and state, their political character and administration is made subservient to the theocratical or religious element. They delight to call their system of government, a "Theo-Democracy;" and that, in a civil capacity, they stand as the Israelites of old under Moses. For the rule of those not fully imbued with the spirit of obedience, and sojourners not of the faith, as well as for things purely temporal, tribunals of justice, and law-making assemblies, are at present rendered necessary. But the rules and regulations vouchsafed from the throne of Heaven are fixed and unchangeable, which have preceded all present necessities, and by them are they guided in the manner of providing for, and executing temporal affairs: — so that those holding the revelations of God's Will, are the ones who make laws according to Truth, and the rulers or executors are clothed in Righteousness, and the end is Peace. In fact, their President of the church is the temporal civil governor, *because* he is the Seer of the Lord, and rules in virtue of that prophetic right over the home and Catholic "Latter-Day Saints of the Church of Jesus Christ," usually styled the Mormons. And should one be assigned to them, not of their creed, or other than their chief, he would find himself without occupation. He probably would be received with all due courtesy as a distinguished personage, cordially received in social intercourse so long as his demeanor pleased the influential members and people: — but as Governor — to use their own expressive phrase,—"he would be let severely alone." Were he to convoke an assembly, and order an election, no attention would be paid to it, and he would be subjected to the mortification of seeing a legislature, chosen at a different time, enacting statutes, or else the old ones continued, and those laws enforced and the cases arising from their conflict adjudicated, by the present tribunals of justice, under their own judges. This certainly has been proclaimed as their determined policy, though there might arise circumstances that would cause them to dissemble for a time; and the peaceful character of the people would be assigned as the reason why no other burden was thrown upon foreign functionaries than the labor of drawing their salaries from the distant treasury. The dignity and the form of courts might easily obtain, to which Gentile sojourners or emigrants could resort, but the members of the Latter-Day Church would know nothing about them; their causes are to be settled in the church and not go to law out of it. The church is the court for doctrinal error — for other offences they have the statutes of Deserét, and what they call "Common Mountain Law."

For, among themselves, all disputes are to be settled under a "church" organization, to which is attached the civil jurisdiction, with officers, from the inferior justice of the peace up to the Governor. But the justice is a Bishop of a ward in the city or precinct of the town or county; the Judges on the bench of the superior courts are constituted from the High Priests, from the quorums of seventies, or from the college of the Apostles; and the Seer is the highest ruler and consulting Judge. A double name is therefore required, by which the same persons execute the functions in their different official capacities, according as they relate to prescribed civil or spiritual matters, except on opinions, or purity of faith. Even the legislature can make no law upon, or regulating what is given in "Revelations" to the prophet, only so far as is necessary to carry them into effect in social transactions.

The entire management is under the Presidency, which consists of three persons, the Seer and two counsellors. It is this board that governs their universal church; called universal because they claim to have preached in almost every nation, and in the United States in each congressional district; and have gathered societies called "Stakes of Zion," arranged on the model of their home assembly, on the islands of the ocean and either continent—and all are to obey the Presidency; at home in all things, and abroad in spiritual things, independent of every consideration—and the converts are commanded "to gather, gather, gather to the mountains," as fast as convenient and compatible with their character and situation. They have made an exception in favor of the Pacific islanders, of whom they claim to have many thousands, whose effeminacy and habits unfit them for the labors and rugged climate of the rocky land; to whom several American families have been sent, to reside among and superintend them.

The number of inhabitants in the mountains has been greatly over-estimated, but there are probably in Utah and on the frontiers of the states, ready to move up the coming year, about thirty thousand; and the number is fast increasing by the influx from England, Wales, and from the continent of Europe; every possible effort is made to bring up the emigrants, and swell the numerical strength to a position that can demand the independent place of a state in the Union — great inducement is held out, by guaranteeing wages for a fixed term of years to all superior and practical workmen in textile fabrics, in cutlery and machinery, no matter what shall be their religious belief.

ORIGIN OF THE MORMON CHURCH.

This people are there under assumed prophetic direction, and it is not amiss to glance at their origin, and the means by which this late desert and solitary wilderness is now blossoming under the hand of this peaceful, industrious, and harmonious community.

The founder of the Mormon Sect was Joseph Smith, a native of Vermont, who emigrated when quite young in his father's family to Western New-York. According to his autobiography, published in a series of letters, he was of a religious turn of mind, and, when seventeen years of age, became greatly interested in the "revivals of religion," often occurring among the "denominations" in that section of country. In one of these times his feelings were so powerfully wrought upon that he gave himself up to continued prayer for some days — and meditating still at night, he at length arose while all the family were hushed in sleep, and poured forth his soul, "agonizing" to have made known to him the truth, among the conflicting opinions he heard by the various sects. His apartment became suddenly illuminated, and an angel appeared and conversed familiarly with him, and instructed him in the way of righteousness; informing him also that there was no true church upon the earth. The doctrine taught on this point is, that the church which was once established, had fallen under the rule given by the prophet, and had "changed the ordinances," "broken the everlasting covenant," and "corrupted the faith;" for which cause it was removed from earth—or, in their figurative expression, "the man child was caught up into heaven," which means that the priesthood was taken away fifteen hundred years ago. And Joseph was told that his prayers were heard and registered in the books on high, and that, being dearly beloved of the Lord, he should be commissioned a priest after the order of Melchisedek, and restore that line among men, organizing a church of faithful persons, to receive the Lord in the Millennium, which time should be hastened according to their degree of *mighty faith*, for he was determined "to cut the work short in righteousness." In after visits he was further instructed that "truth should spring out of the earth"—(Ps.)—and that, accordingly, he should be conducted to the hill Cumorra, in Palmyra, New York, and receive from out the ground holy and prophetic records concerning a family of Jews that emigrated from Jerusalem in the time of Zedekiah, and were miraculously led to America, across the eastern ocean.

On being guided to the spot, he found a square stone box, eight inches high, covered with a slab, cemented upon it; and made repeated trials to open it. He was struck back by an invisible blow, and informed, in answer to his earnest prayer, that the want of success was owing to his listening to the suggestions of Satan, who had walked at his elbow on the way, and had made him resolve to make use of the golden plates on which the records were engraved, as well as the contents when published, to advance his temporal fortunes. This was sin—to think he should become famous was unholy ambition; that he should be rich and powerful thereby, was avarice.

But, on sincere repentance and submission, four years after, the contents of the box were shown to him, the angel opening it; which consisted of the "Sword of Laban," brought from Jerusalem, a breastplate and two stones, "bright and shining," and golden plates engraved with characters, and united at the backs by rings. A portion of the records was received, constituting the Book of Mormon, in which are depicted, much in the style of the Bible Chronicles, the various fortunes of the four brothers of the emigrating family, and of their descendants — how some tribes were evil in their practices, despising reproof, and became cursed with a dark skin and loathsome habits, and were made scourges to others when falling away from the truth — the sayings, teachings, and warnings of their prophets, who foretold by name the advent of the Savior of the world — the organization among the purer people on this continent, of a church by Christ, who came down to them after his ascension at Jerusalem, and gave them his gospel nearly in the words of the Sermon on the Mount, and how that for apostasy these Christians were finally destroyed by the Gadianton robbers and the red men — the last prophet, Moroni by name, sealing up the Records, and depositing them, with the sword, Urim and Thummim, and breastplate, at Cumorah, there to remain until "the fullness of time" should demand their exhumation; and which should be brought forth, "by way of Gentile," for the "convincing of both Jew and Gentile that Jesus is the Christ." (See Preface, B. Mormon.)

The restoring angel was the spirit of this same Moroni, the son of Mormon the Seer, who had made a compendium of the holy writings and delivered them to him; and Joseph, now constituted the Seer, by means of the Urim and Thummim, placed in a bow and looked through upon the plates, began their translation, and preached the news of his important mission. A convert, named Cowdery, baptized him, it being so commanded by the angel, in order that a beginning should be made; and the prophet then baptized his convert. At this ceremony in the woods of Pennsylvania, in the clear Susquehannah, or one of its branches, there were present, to approve of this necessity, and by their sanctions remit irregularity, the angels or spirits of Moses and Elias of the old dispensation; as also Peter, James, and John of the new.* In 1830 the first organization was made in Manchester, New York, and that is the Epoch of the New Church of the Latter-Day Saints. Revelations were made to Joseph, and certain men were designated by the revelator for missionary labor, and converts increased; or, as one of the members of that day, and an apostle now, said, "the word of the Lord greatly grew and magnified, and many were obedient to the faith" — and soon we find that at Kirtland, Ohio, a temple was in process of building.

But, for certain reasons, hereafter to be developed, this place was abandoned, and a spot designated by revelation in Missouri, was declared to be intended for them, as their inheritance — for

---

* Book Doc. and Cov. 27.

"there was the New Jerusalem to be built by the saints, after a pattern sent down from heaven, and upon the spot where the garden of Eden bloomed, and Adam was formed." The altar on which Adam did sacrifice, was shown to Joseph, at least some of the stones of which it was built; and, on the north side of the river, a city was located in the place where Adam blessed his children.

In that state, cruel persecutions followed — driven from Zion, they took refuge in adjoining counties — and again crimes of a dark dye were alleged against them; the leaders were imprisoned for treason, and they aver that in one jail they were furnished with human flesh for food: the flesh of their own slaughtered comrades. They suffered greatly; and finally, expelled by force of law and the mob, they took refuge in Illinois, and began the building of a temple in the city of Nauvoo; a city which in a few years had twenty thousand inhabitants. But, though caressed for a time, they fell under suspicion, as they allege, most unjustly, on account of the flocking in of horse-thieves and counterfeiters, who carried on secretly their nefarious plans, as in other towns; and all the crimes committed in the country around were maliciously attributed to them. It ended in the murder of Joseph, the Seer, and Hyrum, the Patriarch, by the mob at Carthage jail, in 1844, and the re-organization of the major part of the society, under Brigham Young, as the Lord's Prophet and Seer to the saints, to receive the revelations for them in a church capacity, with the title of First President.

A temporary lull ensued in the tempest of persecution, but the storm gathered force again. Such threats were made, that it was necessary to seek another home. A prophecy having been made by the present venerable patriarch, and the uncle of the late seer, that they must retire to the wilderness and endure perils and tribulations for a time, before their final triumph over their foes, a delegation was dispatched to the mountains; and Salt Lake Valley was selected, in the far-off California of Mexico, as a resting place.

SETTLING SALT LAKE VALLEYS.

Under the conduct of "Brigham the Seer" a colony of 4000 persons was planted there in 1847;—the Presidency arrived on the 24th of July, which day was one of joy and gladness, and its anniversaries are to be held in great esteem, and celebrated with rejoicings evermore. In five days a large tract was ploughed, planted with potatoes, and the city-creek dammed, and irrigating ditches filled; and the spot on which they first rested being the most eligible site in the valley, a city was immediately laid out. A fort enclosing about forty acres, was built, by facing log-houses inward, and picketing four gateways on each side of the square, making a line nearly a mile and a half in length—the timber being hauled several miles, and cut in the distant kanyons.

The land was consecrated by solemn ceremonies to the Lord and his saints, and a permanent location made on territory, to which none of the wandering tribes of Indians could show a title, which they thought of such validity, that they ought to purchase it, or make remuneration to them for its occupancy.

During the following year, every month was so mild that they ploughed and sowed in each,—but though the winter was auspicious and all things so favorable, they were so reduced in provisions as to eat the hides of the slaughtered animals, and eagerly searched them out of the ditches, and tore them from the roofs of the houses, to boil them for the table, and they dug side by side with the miserable Utes for the wild roots used by them for food. But the most formidable enemy they had to contend with, as the crops were nearing maturity, was the army of black, ungainly crickets —"a frightful bug," as a Liverpool sojourner called it when first he saw one:—which, descending from the mountain-sides, destroyed every green herb in their way. In vain did the sorrowful farmers surround their fields with trenches, and fill them with water; the black host, leaping in, floated over, and with wonderful instinct, kept on the course of march, and mounting up the wheat-stalk, would cut it off at the curve which was bent by the weight of the fruit more precious than golden seeds. Whole families might be seen standing guard, with branches and boards in their hands, uttering loud shouts, and endeavoring to turn back and beat off the invaders. In some instances, they succeeded in changing the direction of the march along the streams, and destroyed many in the waters, but it was only a partial relief on a few points of attack.

But better defenders soon came to their aid. These were the most beautiful birds of the valley, the glossy white gulls, with bright red beaks and feet; dovelike in form and motion, with plumage of downy texture and softness. After the first moulting of the crickets, they came in flocks to feast on the banquet which was so bountifully spread for their reception. In early dawn, they rise from the nesting islands of the Great Lake and gliding through the air, gracefully alight on the smooth and gentle slopes at the last of the terraces at the mountains' base, and feast the livelong day.

Luxurious like their Roman prototypes, when filled to satiety, they disgorge the meal, and return with renewed appetites to the plentiful repast; and just as the sun touches the highest mountain-peaks in the ranges of the Great Salt Desert to the West, they expand their long wings, and soar away in countless multitudes to their insular retreats, secure from molestation. A few vigilant sentinels pass to and fro during the day, watchful of the callow young; caring for their wants, and conveying intelligence seemingly to the old and the young, at home and abroad, that "all 's well." Since that season, the crops of the Mormons have amply met their wants; protection to their fields is more perfect, and the assiduous gulls continue their annual visit, which at first was supposed miraculous; and for the three past years there has been a surplus of food, which was sold to the gold emigrants at a less price than at fort Laramie, four hundred miles nearer the States.

Their admirable system of combining labor, while each has his own property, in land and tenements, and the proceeds of his industry, the skill in dividing off the lands, and conducting the irrigating canals to supply the want of water, which rarely falls between April and October,—the cheerful manner in which every one applies himself industriously, but not laboriously:— the complete reign of good neighborhood and quiet in house and fields, form themes for admiration to the stranger coming from the dark and sterile recesses of the mountain gorges into this flourishing valley: — and he is struck with wonder at the immense results, produced in so short a time by a handful of individuals.

This is the result of the guidance of all those hands by one master mind; and we see a comfortable people residing where, it is not too much to say, the ordinary mode of subduing and settling our wild lands could never have been applied.

To accomplish this, there was required religious fervor, with the flame fanned by the breezes of enthusiasm—the encircling of bands into the closest union, by the outward pressure of persecution — the high hopes of laying up a prospective reward, and returning to their deserted homes in great prosperity — the belief of re-enacting the journey of the Israelitish church under another Moses, through the Egypt already passed, to arrive at another Jerusalem, more heavenly in its origin, and beautiful in its proportions and decorations.

Single families on that line of travel would have starved or fallen by the treachery of the Sioux, the cunning of the Crows and Shoshones, or the hatred of the savage Utahs. Concert and courage of the best kind were required and brought into the field, and the result is before us — to their own minds as the direct blessing and interposition of Providence, to others the natural reward of associated industry and perseverance.

Four other colonies have branched off from this parent one, and cities with thickly populated and rapidly growing suburbs, extend on a line of two hundred miles, from Box Elder creek on the north, to the Little Salt Lake on the south, and thence towards San Diego: at the turn of the Nevada Mountain, a *rancho* has been purchased and a station made, soon to be followed by others; whereby a chain of posts will be established for the convenience of receiving their emigration by way of a seaport on the Pacific.

The Great Salt Lake City was laid out into squares in 1847; the streets are one hundred and thirty-two feet wide, with twenty feet side-walks, and the City creek divided to run along each walk and water a colonnade of trees, and also to be led into the gardens. The lots contain each nearly an acre, and face on alternate streets with eight lots in each block.

The site is on a scarcely perceptible slope, except the northern part, which rises upon the first natural terrace, and lies in the angle of the main Wahsatch range, running north and south, and a giant spur that makes out directly to the west, and terminates one half mile from the Jordan River. The city is four miles square, and touches the river bank on the west side. It can be watered by several creeks, and a canal twelve miles long, to cross three other streams, is constructed; to bring the Big Cottonwood along the eastern terrace to the present capital of this new empire.

Forty miles north is Ogden City, beautifully located near the junction of Ogden and Weber rivers—and sixty miles south is another plat, soon to be occupied, on the Timpanogos; and thence one hundred and thirty miles in the same direction, is the city of Manti, and settlement of the San Pete Valley. Paroan, or Iron City, so named from the abundance of ore, and facilities for procuring fuel for their furnaces, is in the valley of the Little Salt Lake, where it is reported that a much larger body of irrigable land is found than in that first settled.

In Tuilla Valley, thirty miles west of the temple, is a settlement; and there are now in successful operation ten saw and five grist mills, and others erecting in all the newer locations. A large, commodious state-house was completed in 1850; and a wooden railway laid to the Red Butte quarries, four miles distant, for transporting the fine red sandstone to the Temple Block, where a gorgeous pile is to be erected, which shall surpass in magnificence any yet built by man, and which shall be second only to that finally to be constructed by themselves, when the Presidency shall be installed at the New Jerusalem, on the temple site of Zion.

To the north of Temple Block, and close by, towers up and overlooks the Temple City, the "Ensign Mound." It terminates the great spur, and is conspicuous in approaching the city, from every quarter. On this mountain peak there is soon to be unfurled the most magnificent flag ever thrown to the breeze, constructed out of the banner flags of all peoples. Joined in symbolical unity, "the flag of all nations" shall wave above the sacred temple; then shall they verify the decree given by the Prophet Isaiah—(ch. ii. 18, 25.)—"All ye inhabitants of the world and dwellers upon earth, see ye, when he lifteth up an ensign upon the mountains—and he will lift up an ensign to the nations from far, and will hiss unto them from the end of the earth—and it shall come to pass in the last days that the mountain of the Lord's house shall be established in the tops of the mountains, and shall be exalted above the hills, and all nations shall flow into it."

Their comparative comfort and degree of prosperity is significantly shown by the fact that they canvassed the country, to ascertain how many inmates there would be for a poor-house, and finding only two disposed to ask public bounty, they concluded that it was not yet time to build a house of charity: and this among the thousands who, three years before, were deprived of their property, and could, with the utmost difficulty, transport their families into the valley.

CHAPTER III.

SPIRITUAL CLAIMS OF THE MORMONS.

SUCH then is the outward appearance of this separate people. But it is not enough in this enquiring age to portray merely their external condition, and the country they inhabit.

They claim to be "separate and peculiar" on higher and different grounds, than worldly prosperity and human laws; — and those pretensions, with the consequent action, have called forth much vain and erroneous speculation, from not fully comprehending the principles which give rise to their conduct, in their relations to other communities and individuals. The pretension is, that they constitute the only true Church of God and His Son, and their hopes rest upon the expectation of the intervention soon of the King of Kings, by which, under the guidance of the Spirit, they shall gather to themselves individually, all who are destined and prepared to listen to the voice of Truth; and then all the sects of Christendom will be absorbed into that one most concentrated and most numerous.

When these two hosts are fairly marshalled, the one under the banner of the Pope of Rome, and "the saints" around the "Flag of all nations," "led by their Seer," wearing the consecrated breastplate, and flourishing the glittering golden sword of Laban, delivered him by angelic hands, from their long resting-place; then shall be fought the great battle, mystically called, of Gog and Magog: — the Lord contending for his people with fire, pestilence, and famine; and in the end, the earth will become the property of the Saints, and He will descend from His heavenly throne to reign over them through a happy Millennium.

During the preparations for those battles, to be more fierce than man ever yet has fought, the Jews will be erecting another temple at the Palestine Jerusalem, on which their long-expected Sa vior will stand and exhibit Himself in the conquering brightness that they supposed he would bear at the first appearance, and their hearts will be bowed as one man to receive Him, with repentant humility for the past, and glorious joy for the future, and the city will rise in great magnificence;—and the New Israelites of America will have their head-quarters of the Presidency in Jackson County, Missouri, where they will build up the New Jerusalem, the joy of the whole earth; and, at the presence of the Lord of Majesty, the land which "*was divided*" in the days of Noah into continents and islands, shall be "*Beulah, married*" and become one entirely as at the original creation,—and, from these two cities, villas and habitations shall extend in one continuous neighborhood, among which shall prevail entire concord: no one will have the disposition to rebel or be allowed to act against the harmony of the whole.

And there shall be "thrown up," between the two Jerusalems "the highway on which the lion hath not trod, and which the eagle's eye hath not seen"—then the temple described by Ezekiel will be erected in all its particulars for the exercise of the functions of the two priesthoods,—for the Aaronic, held by the tribe of Levi, who will return to their duties and renew animal sacrifices; and for the Melchisedek, the greater priesthood, held by those commissioned through Joseph the Seer.

At the end of the Millennium, those who have not been sincere in their obedience to the Lord's reign will be permitted to show their rebellious spirit a short time under the direction of their captain Satan; and at last be overwhelmed with destruction from the presence of the good:—and the Earth, which is believed to be a creature of life, will be celestialized and gloriously beautified for the meek and pure in heart.

Such is a summary outline of their claims and expectations, but the preaching from the pulpit, and extempore teachings, are usually confined to the promulgation of doctrines like those commonly taught by the Christian sects which hold to Faith, Repentance, Baptism, and the Resurrection of the Body.

Their mode of conducting worship is to assemble at a particular hour, and the senior priest then indicates order by asking a blessing on the congregation and exercises — when a hymn from their own collection is sung, prayer made extempore, and another sacred song, followed by a sermon from some one previously appointed to preach; which is usually continued by exhortations and remarks from those who "feel moved upon to speak." Then notices of the arrangement of the tithe labor for the ensuing week, and information on all secular matters, interesting to them in a church capacity, is read by the council clerk, and the congregation dismissed by a benediction.

While the congregation is assembling and departing from the house, it is usual for the large and excellent band of music to perform anthems, marches, and waltzes, which drives away all sombre feelings, and prepares the mind for the exciting and often eloquent discourses. As there are a large number of Welsh in the meetings, and many of them not understanding the English language, a version of the principal discourse is sometimes made to them by an interpreter, and a Welsh choir will then exhilarate all present by singing one of their hymns, to one of their charming, wild, romantic airs.

We will now open up the view of their particular doctrines, first premising that what is here stated is drawn from the perusal of some of their accredited books, and heard in their pulpit preaching — or obtained in free conversation with their well-instructed and principal men. Nor would I, in the least, wish to misrepresent the doctrines themselves, or abuse any confidence of the friends, whom I feel justified to call such, among them, on account of their kindness, oftentimes shown in circumstances to be appreciated. Many points were elicited by direct interrogation, and others obtained from the oral discourses on the preacher's stand — and as it was a common thing for the speakers, when not of the Presidency, to appeal to their superiors, who sat behind them to correct any thing mistaken for the teaching of the Holy

Spirit, through their mouths; all such doctrines we suppose to be adopted as true which were suffered to go unrebuked. That most of this exposition is the constant subject of teaching, we by no means affirm — as in all Christian sects, it is seldom that abstruse themes are discussed before a promiscuous audience—the principal part of this *theology* is the "strong meat" reserved for those who have been fed on the milk, as weaker members.

We first introduce an article taken from the paper called the Frontier Guardian, edited by Orson Hyde, of the Apostolic College, and I believe at the head of it, giving the faith of the Latter-Day Saints.

CHAPTER IV.

LATTER-DAY SAINTS' FAITH.

"We believe in God the eternal Father, and his son Jesus Christ, and in the Holy Ghost.

We believe that men will be punished for their own sins, and not for Adam's transgressions.

We believe that through the atonement of Christ all mankind may be saved, by obedience to the laws and ordinances of the Gospel.

We believe that these ordinances are — 1st. Faith in the Lord Jesus Christ: 2d. Repentance: 3d. Baptism by immersion for the remission of sins: 4th. Laying on of hands for the gift of the Holy Spirit: 5th. The Lord's Supper.

We believe that men must be called of God by inspiration, and by laying on of hands from those who are duly commissioned to preach the Gospel, and administer in the ordinances thereof.

We believe in the same organization that existed in the primitive church, viz: apostles, prophets, pastors, teachers, evangelists, &c.

We believe in the powers and gifts of the everlasting gospel, viz: the gift of faith, discerning of spirits, prophecy, revelation, visions, healing, tongues, and the interpretation of tongues, wisdom, charity, brotherly love, &c.

We believe the word of God recorded in the Bible, we also believe the word of God recorded in the Book of Mormon, and in all other good books.

We believe all that God has revealed, all that he does now reveal, and we believe that he will reveal many more great and important things pertaining to the kingdom of God and Messiah's second coming.

We believe in the literal gathering of Israel, and in the restoration of the ten tribes, that Zion will be established upon the western continent, that Christ will reign personally upon the earth a thousand years, and that the earth will be renewed, and receive its paradisaical glory.

We believe in the literal resurrection of the body, and that the rest of the dead live not again until the thousand years are expired.

We claim the privilege of worshipping Almighty God according to the dictates of our conscience, unmolested, and allow all men the same privilege, let them worship how or where they may.

We believe in being subject to kings, queens, presidents, rulers, and magistrates; in obeying, honoring, and sustaining the law.

We believe in being honest, true, chaste, temperate, benevolent, virtuous, and upright, and in doing good to all men; indeed, we may say that we follow the admonition of Paul, we "believe all things," we "hope all things," we have endured very many things, and hope to be able to "endure all things." Every thing lovely, virtuous, praiseworthy, and of good report, we seek after, looking forward "to the recompense of reward." But an idle or lazy person cannot be a Christian, neither have salvation. He is a drone, and destined to be stung to death and tumbled out of the hive."

The books regarded as authoritative with them, and which give a fuller illustration are — The Book of Mormon — Doctrines and Covenants — Voice of Warning — The Gospel Reflector — The Times and Seasons, edited under the eye of the Prophet — The Millennial Star — and the writings of Joseph the Seer and Parley P. Pratt, wherever found; and the "General Epistles of the Presidency in Deserét."

We will not take up this seriatim, but remark, that it is only when we come to the definition of terms, that the peculiarities of belief will appear in their theology. They believe in the sacred character of the Bible, but what interpretations do they give to its pages? – they believe in God, but what is the character assigned to the Deity?—they adopt the Sacraments, but of what efficacy and application to Salvation?

Of the Bible it is taught, that in the main we have a correct translation of that given by Inspiration in the version called King James';— but that there have been many interpolations by design of the corrupters of Christianity, and many misunderstandings of several passages. These have all been corrected by Joseph the Seer, to whom was given "the key of all languages,"—or as he says in The Last Sermon, the one he preached at Nauvoo, and which was reported by some one and printed after his death, "I know more than all the world put together, and the Holy Ghost within me comprehends more than all the world, and I will associate with it,"—and thus having direct inspiration to do this work, the emendated book is prepared and is soon to be printed. As a specimen of the alterations on this vital subject, we quote from the same paper as above; "I will make a comment on the very first sentence of the history of the creation in the Bible. It first read, 'The head one of the Gods brought forth the Gods.' If you do not believe it, you do not believe *the learned* man of God. And in further explanation it is observed that it means, The Head God called together the Gods, and sat in grand council. The grand counsellors sat in yonder heavens, and contemplated the worlds that were created at that time.' The Bible is therefore held to be the *foundation book*, but instead of taking it in the usual sense, there must be a certain change of meaning in the most important point, which will be elaborated when we speak concerning the Deity. But when it is read, it is to be taken in its most literal sense and they most pointedly condemn those who spiritualize its contents, saying that God is honest when he speaks with man, and uses words in their literal acceptation and 'never palters in a double sense.'" But the Word of God is held to be not confined to this one Book, and, of others in existence, they take of equal authority the Book of Mormon, and "Doctrines and Covenants." The latter is composed of a lecture on Faith in six sections, written by Rigdon, though published in the name of the Prophet, and several

Revelations to the Seer and Revelator; and these books are claimed to be a "three-fold cord" agreeing in sentiment and purpose, and unfolding the dealings of God toward man and the church Additional revelations are made from day to day according to th exigences of the people and church; and this is assigned as the reason why they are so far in advance of the Christian world in spiritual, heavenly knowledge, and causes them to sneer upon all who adhere alone to the old revelations, and to pity them for their blindness and ignorance. "A flood of light has poured into their souls and raised them to a view of the glorious things above"— and Development may be called the distinguishing feature of their church. The Rock on which the church is founded is by them declared to be Revelation. And it was on what "*had been revealed* to Peter" that the church was to rest:—in other words we may state their doctrine to be, that Revelation, which is now with them, is the Rock of the Church of Christ.

"Thus saith the Lord * * * * * my son thou art blessed henceforth, that bear the keys of the kingdom given unto you"— "verily I say unto you, the keys of this kingdom shall never be taken from you, while thou art in the world"—"And * * I give unto you a commandment, that you continue in the ministry and Presidency, and when you have finished the translation of the prophets you shall from henceforth preside over the affairs of the church and the schools, and from time to time, as shall be manifest from the Comforter, receive revelations to unfold the mysteries of the kingdom, and set in order, and study and learn and become acquainted with all good books, and with languages, tongues, and people." This extract from the Revelation given in 1833 and found in the Book of Covenants, page 329, is here inserted to show the character of such heavenly communications and authority for my statements. They will allow that their Revelations are contradictory to each other, but that is explained by the different "circumstances" under which they are given; "heaven's government is conducted on the principle of adapting revelation to the varied circumstances of the children of the kingdom."

DEITY.

Let us now return to the consideration of the article first named in the Latter-Day Saints' Faith concerning the Deity. The Supreme Hierarchy that is worshipped and invoked is a Trinity or rather a duality of Persons.

"God the Father," is held to be a man perfected: but so far advanced in the attributes of his nature, his *faith*, intelligence and power, that in comparison with us, He may be called The Infinite.

The "Son, Jesus Christ," is the offspring of the Father by the Virgin Mary. The eternal Father came to the earth, and wooed and won her to be the wife of his bosom. He sent his herald-angel Gabriel to announce espousals of marriage, and the Bridegroom and bride met on the plains of Palestine, and the Holy Babe that was born was the "tabernacle" prepared for and assumed by the Spirit-Son, and that now constitutes a God.

"The Holy Ghost" is the concomitant will of both The Father and The Son; the one mind possessed and acting in each, which produces universal harmony of thought, wisdom, and being, throughout their dominions. The Spirit differs from the Father and Son, in being merely a Spiritual Soul or Existence, which has never taken a tabernacle, that is, a material body as the Gods have, and has not therefore died, after passing the period of probation, and thence through the Resurrection to perfection.

In this statement I have endeavoured to give their true teaching, and do not intend to criticise or explain any apparent contradictions. The authority for the first two propositions is found in the Last Sermon of their great prophet, which relieves me, in a measure from the pain of stating them,—but facts and principles are here involved on which the candor and judgment of the reader must be exercised. What is influencing the life-philosophy of hundreds of thousands is not a thing of slight importance, or to be misstated with impunity.

"First, God himself, who sits enthroned in yonder heavens, is a man like unto one of yourselves, that is the great secret. If the vail was rent to-day, and the great God who holds this world in its orbit, and upholds all things by his power, if you were to see him to-day, you would see him in all the person, image, and very form as a man; for Adam was created in the very fashion and image of God; Adam received instruction, walked, talked, and conversed with him, as one man talks and communes with another." * * * "I am going to tell you how God came to be God. God himself, the Father of us all, dwelt on an earth, the same as Jesus Christ himself did, and I will show it from the Bible. Jesus said, as the Father hath power in himself, even so hath the Son power; to do what? why, what the Father did, that answer is obvious: in a manner to lay down his body and take it up again. Jesus, what are you going to do? — To lay down my life as *my Father did*, and take it up again."

There is a quotation extant from the author of the "Voice of Warning," to the effect that "we worship a God who hath both body and parts; who has eyes, mouth, and ears, and who speaks when, and to whom he pleases—who is just as good at mechanical inventions as at any other business."

But we are referred by their teachers to the Apocalypse, where it is written of the redeemer: "And hath made us kings and priests unto God and *his Father*;" and to the Apostle that said, "there are gods many and lords many," to prove that the Father had "*his Father*," and they talk boldly of the grandfather, great-grandfather of God, thus tracing back almost *ad infinitum* to the "Head God, that called the grand council together when the worlds came rolling into existence." We, however, have only to limit our worship, and obey our Heavenly Father and His Son, who are revealed to us by the Spirit; and "when we know how to come to him, he is ready to come to us and unfold the heavens to our knowledge." The Son (when a spirit) took of the unformed "chaotic matter; element which had an existence from the time God had, and in which dwells all the glory," and formed our earth and the planetary world, peopled, and has redeemed it. He is to be worshipped as Lord of all, and heir of the Father in power, creation, and dominion. "What did Jesus do?—why, I do the things that I saw my Father do when worlds came rolling into existence—I saw my Father work out his kingdom with fear and trembling, and I must do the same." (Last Sermon, p. 61.)

So of each man, whose spirit hath the same Father—by obedience and faith he may be perfected, and attain to the power of forming a planet, peopling and redeeming it, over which he may reign forever. And all who do not obey the *revelations* now sent to them, and properly fulfil their probation, will only succeed to an inferior glory and be permitted to act as servants, "hewers of wood and drawers of water," in some one of the King Saints' Kingdoms; just fitted to the "glory" they have lived for, or such as their vicious lives will allow. In reply to the question, what will you do for us?—they will say, we may make you bootblack or kitchen scullion, or if you behave pretty well and not molest the saints, you may be raised to butler or baker, and carry the train, on state occasions, of our queens in paradise. Things on earth, and customs and ceremonies, are patterned after things in heaven, and will be continued in the spirit world and future abodes of the gods. Their prophet thus instructs the faithful—"You have got to learn to be gods yourselves; to be kings and priests to God; the same as all the gods have done, by going from one small degree to another, from grace to grace, from exaltation to exaltation, until you are able to sit in glory, as doth those who sit enthroned in everlasting power." And in seeking for a place in the eternal worlds, we are informed that there are four different glories to strive for; the celestial, or highest, the telestial, the terrestrial, and lake of fire—of the sun, of the stars, of the earth, and the burning caldron.

SACRAMENTS.

The Book of Covenants teaches that baptism is duly administered by being fully immersed in the water, and that any other manner of applying the element is a vain ceremony. Baptism, legally partaken of, is for remission of sins; sins only forgiven in baptism. The further peculiarity of the subject consists in a vicarious immersion of living persons for their dead friends, who have never had the opportunity, or neglected it when living. This is called "Baptism for the Dead." There being, according to their view, a probationary state in the spiritual world, while that on earth exists, so that by proxy one can fulfil all "righteousness," by submitting to all prescribed rites, of which baptism is one—it is presumed that those gone before have repented, and are now desirous of baptistic benefits; and hence it is enjoined that the "greatest responsibility that God has laid on us is to look after our dead;" and ordered, that a man be baptised for deceased relatives, tracing back the line to one that held the priesthood among his progenitors, who, being a saint, will then take up the place of sponsor, and relieve him of further responsibility. All those who are thus admitted to salvation will be added to the household of the baptized person at the resurrection, who will then prefer his claim, or do as our Lord did at the grave of Lazarus, and call them forth in the name of Jesus; over whom, he, as the most distinguished of the line, will reign as patriarch for ever; and his rank and power among kingly saints will be in proportion to the number of his retinue.

The authority for this application of the rite is grounded on the interrogatory of the Apostle: "Else what shall they do which are baptized for the dead, if the dead rise not at all? why are they then baptized for the dead?"—and Joseph observes in his sermon, "Every man who has got a friend in the eternal world can save him, unless he has committed the unpardonable sin, so you can see how far you can be a Savior;" the Apostle says, "they without us cannot be made perfect."

The child begins its accountability at eight years of age; up to that time the parents are responsible, but then they must have it baptized into the church; and infant baptism is held to be an abomination and a sin. Regeneration is begun in baptism, and perfected by the laying on of hands, by which the recipient is baptized by the Holy Ghost through the Melchisedek priesthood.

The Sacrament of the Communion is done, for a "remembrance of the body and blood of The Son," that they may always remember him and keep his commandments, and that "they may have his Spirit to be with them." This is according to the Book of Mormon, and bread and wine are to be used as the symbols. But by a revelation it is forbidden to use the wine made by the Gentiles, and until they can procure the pure juice of the grape from their own cultivation, they use water in place of it, for "it mattereth not what ye shall eat, or what ye shall drink, when ye partake of the Sacrament, if it so be that ye do it with an eye single to my glory;—wherefore ye shall partake of none [wine] except it be made new among you;" and the bread and a pail with a tin or glass vessel to dip the water is carried around among the congregation on their seats, by the bishops, and offered to young and old who generally partake; and this is to be done on every Lord's Day.

After sufficient time has elapsed to build a temple at "Zion" or any appointed stake, "and at Jerusalem, no other places are allowed for the baptisms for the dead." A font will be constructed in the house of the Lord, for these baptisms which were instituted before the foundation of the world—"and elsewhere, saith the Lord your God, they cannot be acceptable unto me, for therein are the keys of the Holy Priesthood ordained, that you may receive honor and glory." (Book of Cov. prophets' Rev.)

The sixth General Epistle instructs the Saints throughout the world to gather home, and pay all tithing dues, that a Temple may be soon completed for the Baptisms of living and dead. It says; "To be prepared for a celestial heaven, they want *the blessings* of The Terrestrial Temple—and if any pass the temple ordinances without having paid all tithe dues, Jesus will at last declare they are thieves and robbers who have climbed up some other than the appointed way; the ordinances of the temple are as necessary for a full salvation as baptism is for a partial salvation;—the voice of the Good Shepherd is, come home," all ye saints.

FAITH.

The teaching upon this article is rather abstruse—but we may perhaps convey its import in a few words, mostly gleaned from the book of Covenants. It seems to be considered an exercise of the will in intelligent beings on matters of belief, for acquiring celestial glory, and accomplishing holy purposes and works. It is "the assurance that men have in the existence of unseen things, and the principle of action in all intelligent beings; without it, both mind and body would be in a state of inactivity"—and, "by faith we receive all temporal and spiritual blessings." But it is not only the principle of action, but of power, in heaven or in earth; for we find that by *faith,* God created the worlds—(Heb. xi. 3.) and by this we understand it to be the principle of power in the bosom of God by which he works:—"and, take this principle or attribute away from the Deity, he would cease to exist." (See Book of Cov. first chapters.)

"God spake, chaos heard, and worlds came into order by reason of the Faith that was in *him*"—he had "*element* and the principles of element, which can never be destroyed, to organize it out of;—and as these aeon atoms are "intelligent on a self-existent principle, which God himself could not create," we must class the aggregate, or bodies of matter, with life and knowledge capable of exercising faith; which view is sustained, in the language of one of the Presidency, namely;—"for all creation is alive, even the earth itself and the minerals and metals and every other thing connected with it;"—and the first lecture on faith has these words in the last paragraph: "Faith, then, is the great governing principle, which has power, dominion, and authority over all things."

THE EVERLASTING GOSPEL.

In the seventh article of Belief this phrase occurs. By it we may understand, according to their interpretation, the same thing as the Laws of Nature, or whatever name is used to express the arrangement of the universal order of things sprung out of the "two self-existent principles of Intelligence and Element, or matter;" and it is The Law under which the primordial Gods came into being. The prophet has not left on record, to my knowledge, the mannei in which the Head God originated. But he says

"God himself could not create himself," and "intelligence exists upon a self-existent principle: it is a spirit from age to age, and there is no creation about it." In conversation with the more philosophical ones, this question of origin came up frequently, and the explanation elicited was one of opinion merely, and deduced by the reason from the principles already taught by authority. It was, that in the *far eternity*, two of the elementary particles of matter met in consultation and *compared intelligences*, and then called in a third Atom to the council, and, united in one will, they became the first power, to which no other could attain as they had the priority; and by uniting more atoms or exercising the power which the combination gave, would thenceforth progress for ever. Under this union arose the plenitude of power, to make and enforce a Law to govern itself and all things. Thus was the Everlasting Gospel constituted the law of nature.. And out of this Intelligence, according to the Law, a God was begotten, not made, and the other Gods sprung from him as children. By the law of universal order, sex was made to exist, coeternally with all moral existence and life, and not only the Kings, but the Queens of heaven derive their origin equally under its mandates. These are the mothers of our spirits and the gods, and of all spiritual existences also; each of which is confined to its proper sphere and in its own order: and these are called and sent as heralds or ministers from one planetary system to another, or to the different orbs in the same system of worlds. A portion of this order, or Law, is what is called the everlasting gospel in the Revelation of St. John, which was in the hand of the angel "flying in the midst of heaven" to proclaim again on earth concerning the Church of Christ; that angel was Moroni, who brought the gospel in its fulness to "Joseph the Seer," and is now preached to men, with the "signs following" that were promised to the Apostles of the Lord.

To the spirits begotten by the Father, (for the mind of man is not created, "God never did have power to create the spirit of man at all—the very idea lessens man in my estimation—I know better;" Last Sermon, p. 62.) a choice is given, either to remain as they are, or to take a material body and "descend below all things," in order to rise above all things, whereby they can obtain a greater glory than they now enjoy, even to the celestial. This explains why we are here in this earthly tabernacle. Each spirit chose to make "the probation," and thus ignoring all of its past existence, is attempting to work out a salvation of immense worth, and attaining to perfection in the attributes of power, dominion, and happiness.

When the spirit takes possession of its tabernacle, which is probably at the quickening of the embryon, the man *is*, or becomes a living soul. Man is therefore a duality. The elements of his composition are gross matter, called the body, and spirit. The latter is also matter, but more refined or elementary, and so constituted as to permeate the former, control and vivify it. It is not visible to mortal eyes without a miracle, nor is it ponderable; it passes through the body as the electric fluid through the earth—it is in reality more substantial than the body, for it cannot be changed or destroyed, it "existed co-equal with God," and could have no beginning, for then it would be possible to have an end—it is as immortal as God himself." (Sermon, p. 62.) The union or fusion of these makes "the living soul," as related by Moses in the creation of Adam—death separates them for a useful purpose, but then the Spirit watches over every particle of its beloved tabernacle, until the fiat of the resurrection is given, when the body shall again "be clothed upon," and perfect man be the result in an eternal soul.

Death was introduced into humanity by the fall or disobedience of Adam, who is the great patriarch, and is he whom the Scripture calls Michael, The Ancient of Days, with hair like wool. But, in their technical phrase, "Adam fell that men might be," and ate the apple under full knowledge of the consequences, and the "Fall" was a matter of previous arrangement in the economy of *probation*. That is, he fell that man, or a mortal body, might be born of woman, and *tabernacles* fitted up for the spirits, as fast as they chose to undertake their probations. And when a spirit does not answer its true intent in one probation, but forfeits its inheritance by sin and evil conduct, then it will have a lower one assigned it at death, and if disobedient still, another, and another, until it shall be brought to the proper subjection, and, yielding to the gospel law, be allowed to retrace its course back in the successive stages to splendor and angelhood.

Thus it is said of their chief Apostle, at present a president of a stake, and a distinguished writer in both politics and their theology, that he fell into doubt as to the truth of the system, and contemplated apostacy. He was saved by the ministry of angels. A heavenly messenger appeared before him and warned him of the danger, and then pronounced upon him the doom of being soon obliged to take a negro tabernacle, unless he should repent and become zealous for the faith delivered to the Latter-Day Saints. This was effectual in frightening him back to duty, for they hold the "Negro is cursed as to the priesthood, and must always be a servant wherever his lot is cast, and therefore shall never attain to anything above a dim shining glory. This part of the human race is the lowest grade. A first descending probation would be that of the Indian — for the red men have been cursed only as to color and indolent habits; and through repentance and obedience, and acceptance of the newly proclaimed gospel, they can be restored to pristine rights and beauty, and become again "a fair and delightsome people," worthy of their origin from the Jews of Palestine. When these grades have not been effectual in subduing the rebellious spirit, a third one would be assigned into the brute species, and a choice taken among them; and when we are tormented by a refractory horse or obstinate ass, it may not be amiss to reflect that they are actuated by an apostate soul, and exemplifying a few of the "human infirmities." However, it is not our purpose here to draw inferences or reconcile any contradictions which may appear in the Mormon teaching.

Man, in the usual acceptation, is a compound being, with a physical, intellectual, and spiritual *nature* — but in the view taken above, he is a duality of *elements*. The intellectual is absorbed into either of the others, according to convenience, though usually confounded with the spiritual; and the chain of reasoning terminates in exalting the physical nature above the other two.

CHAPTER V.

SAME SUBJECT—MASONRY—HIEROGLYPHICS.

Of the introduction of sin, and rise and progress of Satan, we have heard this account given and "proved by their scriptures."

After Adam had fallen from his first estate, a council was held in Heaven, and all the members were present. Among them was He who is emphatically called The Son, and likewise Lucifer, the elder brother, the Son of the Morning, the bright star in glory, and leader of heavenly hosts. The proposition was laid before the council "how man should be saved or redeemed from the state of evil"—and each one called upon to give his method of salvation. When Lucifer was appealed to, he declared that "he would save him *in* his sins"—but Christ answered, "I will save him *from* his sins."

The latter was deemed the true way by the Father, and accepted; whereupon the Son of the Morning took offence and rebelled, with the legions he managed to corrupt, and was therefore cast out of the planetary abode of the Father, and became the great leader of evil spirits, under the name of Satan—but he brought with him many of the noble qualities he ever possessed; is still Milton's "Archangel ruined and a perfect gentleman."

All the meaner temptations and evil arts are practised only by the baser sort of imps, hence some people are very uncharitable in charging all blame upon the "head devil," as they often call him.

The idea they entertain of the personal agency of this "fine gentleman," may be gathered from the anecdotes rife among them of his doings with Sidney Rigdon, who, from being the next in rank to the prophet Joseph, apostatised, through the love of good cheer, and ambition to be head. He had received a great many visits from his angel, as he supposed, and many revelations—but one night while asleep, he was aroused by so mighty a shake, that he was made aware that no ordinary hand was upon him. Indeed, his satanic majesty was fully confessed, for he proceeded to tilt up the bed and handle Sidney most roughly; and then, taking him by the legs, trundled him down the stairs as one would drag a wheelbarrow behind him, without mercy upon the grey head as it thumped every step; and, finally, landing the sufferer in the street, disappeared "*like smoke.*" This treatment was repeated several times, but 'twere of no use to suggest that some human agency, in the shape of a lusty Mormon, had a hand in the work — for they took the precaution to inquire the color of the hair, the cast of countenance, and other unmistakeable marks, by which Joseph had taught them to detect the real Beelzebub, whenever he appeared as an angel of light, or in propria persona.

TONGUES.

This is not the ancient gift, whereby one addressing a people speaking a different language from himself, was enabled to talk in their own words. It is, that persons among themselves, in their enthusiastic meetings, shall be "moved by the spirit" to utter any set of sounds in imitation of words, and, it may be, words belonging to some Indian or other language. The speaker is to know nothing of the ideas expressed, but another, with the "gift of interpretation of tongues," can explain to the astonished audience all that has been said. Any sounds, of course then are a language known to the Lord. If one feels a desire to speak, and has difficulty to bring forth the thoughts of his heart, or what the spirit is about to reveal through him, he must "rise on his feet, lean in faith on Christ, and open his lips, utter a song in such cadence as he chooses, and the spirit of the Lord will give an interpreter, and make it a language."

THE RESURRECTION.

Their peculiar notions of this cannot be appreciated without knowing their views of the Restoration, or restitution of all things spoken of by Isaiah. When God created the *living earth*, he gave the command that the waters gather to *one place*, and the dry land appear; and hence it is inferred that "there was one vast ocean, rolling around one immense body of land, unbroken as to continents and islands; it was one beautiful plain, interspersed with gently rising hills and sloping vales; its climate delightfully varied with heat and cold, wet and dry, crowning the year with productions grateful to men and animals; "while from the flowery plain or spicy grove sweet odors were wafted on every breeze, and all the vast creation of animated being breathed naught but health, peace, and joy."* Over this creation, residing in a well-watered and delicious garden, "Man reigned, and talked face to face with the Supreme, with only a dimming veil between."

But Adam fell, and the earth partook of the curse that followed, and in pain and sorrow sympathised with the disobedient pair, under its load of thorns and thistles — and sin accumulated its guilty deeds in the actions of men, until the Lord comes out in vengeance and cleanses all by water. After the Noachian deluge, in the days of Peleg, "the earth was divided." Not among families was the surface distributed—but a mighty revolution that brought the sea from its place in the north, to interpose between portions of the land rent asunder; and earthquakes and commotions have since separated it into islands and fragments.

The American continent, as the Book of Mormon informs, was shaken to its foundation at the time of the crucifixion; and cities, towns, mountains, and lakes, buried and formed when "the earth writhed in the convulsive throes of agonizing nature."

Men have degenerated since then as well as the earth; — the ancients were worthy to converse with the Lord and angels, and lessons given "to enlarge the heart and expand the soul to its utmost capacity"—far above the smattering of the present worldly wisdom.

But the restoration of all things is at hand; for "he shall send Jesus Christ, whom the heavens must receive, until the times of

* Voice of Warning.

restitution of all things"—and "the voice of one crying in the wilderness — Every valley shall be exalted and every hill be made low,—and mighty revolutions shall begin to restore the face of the earth to its former beauty." (See Voice of Warning.)

In Rev. vi. we find, "every island and mountain were moved out of their places;" in Isaiah, that "the earth shall move out of her place and be like a chased roe"—but after that, "thou shalt no more be termed forsaken, neither shalt thy land any more be termed desolate; but thou shalt be called Hepzibah, and thy land Beulah; for the Lord delighteth in thee and thy land shall be married." And from the whole and varied scriptures, we learn that the continents and islands shall be united in one, as they were in the morn of creation, and the sea shall retire and assemble in its own place as before; and all these scenes shall take place, about the time of the coming of the Lord." The earth restored, and the inhabitants purified, both man and beast, so that they hurt not, nor destroy—and the knowledge of the Lord covering the earth, as the waters the sea," then comes the first resurrection of the body, to reign on this delightful paradise with the Savior a thousand years.

The peculiarity of this resurrection consists in this; the body is the same as before, "*except the blood.*" That will be left out. The Apostle Pratt (from whom we have been quoting,) says that Jesus was the exact pattern of our resurrection. "And Jesus Christ came forth triumphant from the mansions of the dead, possessing the same body which had been born of a woman, which was crucified; but no blood flowed in his veins; for blood was the ***natural life*** in which were the principles of mortality; and a man restored to flesh and blood would be mortal, which was not the case with our Savior:" and he was substantial, for he told his disciples to handle him, and know that he had "*flesh and bones*;" which will be the constitution of all resurrected bodies.

All the seed of Israel are to be raised from the dead, and brought to the land of Judea; the saints of other peoples, gathered to the fair American division; and the Zion by one, and New

Jerusalem by the other saints, will be built with fine stones, and the beauty of all precious things.

One more change only, will be necessary to fit the earth for man's eternal inheritance, which will take place at the end of the thousand years, the great Sabbath of rest and enjoyment. The earth will be celestialized through the baptism of fire — the two cities will be caught up, literally, into heaven, to descend with the Lord God for its light and its temple, and remain for ever on the "new earth" under the bright canopy of the new heavens."

PROPHECIES AND PROPHETIC TIMES.

There is something ingenious, as well as fanciful, in the method of determining prophetic time. For want of the true key, the commentators have hitherto failed in their interpretations of days and years, and the time for the fulfilment of foretold events.

Now God, our Father, dwells on his planet (Kolob) and measures time by its revolutions; one of those revolutions begins and terminates a day, which is equal to one thousand of our years; the authority for which will readily occur to any Sabbath-school scholar or scripture reader.

Being finite, he employs agents to bring and communicate information through his worlds; and all the material agents of light, electricity, and sound, or attributes, are employed in this thing. When an angel is commissioned a messenger to earth, he is taken from the chief planet perhaps, or quite as likely, from some other that circles around it. But an angel in speaking of the time of events, would of course speak of the days and years, or weeks, that are measured by the revolution of his own abode.

These angels are sent to the Seer to communicate what pertains to the interest or the government of the church, or the orders for individuals to act under the direction of the Seer, as missionaries or otherwise. These communications are registered, to be promulgated at the proper moment, according as the members can bear them, for many "would be offended and turn back" if the whole truth was "dashed down in a mass before them."

Individuals receive revelations regarding their own matters, on proper subjects; these are to be obtained "by prayer in mighty faith," but only when natural sagacity, improved by diligence and study, would fail to suggest the desired information, or point out the required course of action; — where God has appointed means, he will not work by miracles.

At baptism the true believer may ask in faith for some particular "spirit," as, for instance, the spirit whereby one can perceive between true and false doctrines; and intuitively divine it when propounded by those who have the authority to speak, yet may have become darkened through unbelief or evil practice, or brought to them by "the false and seducing spirits," which are to abound in the last days, and such a spirit will be given them to guide and direct.

These attendant angels, however, cannot prevent the approach and insinuations of evil spirits, and thus the two kinds are on the right hand and on the left — which accounts for the crooked paths some pretty good men among them often mark out.

PRIESTHOOD.

It is stoutly maintained that the priesthood is necessary to the being, as well as the perfection of a church; and so long as the Aaronic branch is not exercised by the tribe of Levi through unbelief, their Melchisedek order being the greater, have the right to officiate in the lesser offices, and will do so when the proper temple is built; that is, in the animal sacrifices for daily sins of the people. The priestly order receives tithes of all one possesses on entering the church; and the members pay a tenth of all income, and devote a tenth part of their time to the temple and other public works, ever after.

The bishops have charge of the tithe labor, and receive the contributions (or a commutation for labor and produce,) and put the proceeds of industry in the public store-houses; in fine, this order of priests have charge of the temporal matters under the direction of the Presidency.

The Hierarchy of the Mormon Church has many grades of offices and gifts. The first is the Presidency of three persons, which, we were led to understand, answered or corresponded to the Trinity in Heaven, but more particularly to Peter, James, and John, the first presidents of the gospel church.

Next in order is the travelling High Apostolic College of twelve apostles, after the primitive church model, who have the right to preside over the stakes in any foreign country, according to seniority; then the high-priests—priests, elders, bishops, teachers, and deacons — together with evangelists or missionaries of the "three seventies." Each order constitutes a full quorum for the discipline of its members, and transacting business belonging to its action; but appeals lie to higher orders, and the whole church is the final appellate court assembled in general council.

Their Prophets arise out of every grade, and a Patriarch resides at head quarters to bless particular members, after the manner of Jacob and his sons, and that of Israel towards Esau and his brother.

A High Council is selected out of the high-priests, and consists of twelve members, which is in perpetual session to advise the Presidency; in which each is free to give and argue his opinion. The President sums up the matter and gives the decision, perhaps in opposition to a great majority, but to which all must yield implicit obedience; and probably there has never been known, under the present head, a dissent when the "awful nod" has been given, for it is the "stamp of fate and sanction of a god."

This council is eye, ear, and hand to the President — the members are the spies over all matters in the field or the temple, in the social party or the domestic circle. Is any novel opinion broached in conversation, it is brought before the council by any member cognizant of, or who has heard of it, and measures are taken to ferret it out, that the man who uttered it, if he is not sound to the core, may be marked and pounced upon before he is even aware that he is suspected. No wonder that many among them, who are not well advised of the means of acquiring the knowledge, wonder that Brigham is so well "posted up" in what relates to the private history of the numerous persons around him.

In the early arrangement of the affairs of the Mormon church, and when they were accused of raising up a society and people to be governed independent of the state — there was inserted in the Book of Covenants, the following item of belief: "We do not believe it just to mingle religious influence with civil government, whereby one religious society is fostered, and another proscribed in its spiritual privileges, and the individual rights of its members, as citizens, denied."

Yet it is taught that the priesthood is supreme in the state — not in the sense that all human law springs from the standard of right and wrong contained in the revealed word of God, but that this order has the control of the state, and ought to make the civil regulations, because it receives revelations from day to day, and can therefore keep both the temporal and spiritual from clashing, and fulfil the scripture that "the officers shall be peace and exactors righteousness." And in the selection of officers by ballot, the elective franchise is made subservient to a vote for the nominee of the Presidency.

It was related to us in conversation that a delegate was chosen and commissioned for Congress, at a time when it was desirable that he should start suddenly for the seat of government; and that the people were summoned to vote when he was far on the way to the states — his credentials either in his pocket, or sent to him by mail afterward.

They gloried in this *congé d'elire*, and it was averred by prominent men that to vote against any one proposed by the highest authority would be the height of folly. For the council knew what was wanted to be done, and of course what persons were the most suitable to accomplish the work.

But to return to the subject of the priesthood; we are informed they have working signs, and that Masonry was originally of the church, and one of its favored institutions, to advance the members in their spiritual functions. It had become perverted from its designs, and was restored to its true work by Joseph, who gave again, by angelic assistance, the key-words of the several degrees that had been lost; and when he entered the lodges of Illinois, he could work right ahead of the most promoted; for which, through envy, the Nauvoo lodge was excommunicated, or cut off by the Grand Lodge, on account of its own ignorance of the greatest truths and benefits of Masonry.

The priesthood having the different degrees, preferment in them depends on the faithfulness of the aspirant, as judged by those already promoted, and one of the merits is the paying up of all tithe dues. Any one in arrears on this, will find himself blocked materially when the proper buildings for "working" are constructed. Diligence and obedience are thus held out as things to ensure a reward in knowledge and promotions.

Until the great temple is built, much has to be left undone — that structure has to be arranged with regard to this and other institutions of the priestly orders; and the wants of the church at the time will determine the manner, which will be given by direct revelation.

There will be bathing apartments distinct for the priests and priestesses, for the women are to have a part of this office, and are admitted to certain degrees in Masonry as a consequence. Particular ablutions are to be attended to, before appearing to officiate at the altars, and many observances in the manner of offering worship and praise, and performing symbolical rites, will have the conveniences fitted up for them and diligently kept in practice.

And we may close this notice of "*peculiar doctrines*" and special teachings, by a reference to their assertions, that revelations of God's will in His moral teachings, have been made at various times to all nations; and, through tradition, the truth has been transmitted down, so that there is no people, even the heathen, who have not some correct doctrines and moral notions. Therefore we are not to be surprised to find that they have points in common with every belief under heaven, for being guided by the spirit into all truth, they have sifted it out from the mass of error that obscures it; and whatever has been vouchsafed to man, may be considered in their possession.

On this account they claim an advantage over all proselytes of other creeds, in being able to commence with what is agreeable to both parties, and then extend gradually the teaching upon other matters, from the least objectionable topics up to those fully opposed to previous ideas and habits. Thus, with the Eastern nations and South Sea Islanders, they are not called upon to renounce all but one partner; the animal sacrificer will be told he can retain that practice, and so on to the end of the chapter.

SOURCES OF DOCTRINES.

The ecclesiastical student will not fail to remark that Mormonism is an eclectic religious philosophy, drawn from Brahmin mysticism in the dependence of God, the Platonic and Gnostic notion of Eons, or a moving principle in element; Mahomedan sensualism, and the fanaticism of the sects of the early church; and there is the good and evil of Ahrimaism, with the convenient idea of the transmigration of souls, from the Persian.

Nor has its founder altogether confined his attention to the ancient Christian theories or pagan superstitions; and his followers have fallen in with the spiritual philosophy of the day, and added the doctrine of affinities of minds and the sympathy of souls—he has told us that the spirits of the departed dead are angels that return and converse with those who are congenial to them, or they have the privilege, on account of their purity, to receive communications from ghostly realms—and, taking the antithesis of the dicta, that God is perfect man, he makes every perfect man a god—and by tracing the parallel at our leisure, we may discover that the speculations of modern times have here been more or less modified and adopted, those reveries of ingenious but morbid imaginations, given to the speculative world in mellifluous language, and sensuous, captivating descriptions of enjoyments in the existence that succeeds to this, of, too frequently, *self-made* misery.

Between the school of *mental delight*, and the school of the Mormon, there is this difference; the latter acts now upon his theories, and *materializes* them to present use, while the former revels alone in intellectual sensuality, putting off to the future the feast of the palate, the charms for the eye, or absorption in the delights of affianced love — we leave both to reconcile the differences between themselves and the school of moral obedience and true revelation. By sensuality used in this connection, we mean that application of the senses in a lawful manner for procuring desiderated enjoyment, which education and conscience allows to those of any adopted creed.

In Mormonism we recognise an intuition of Transcendentalism — intuitive, we say, for its founder was no scholar in the idealistic philosophy. He trampled under foot creeds and formulas, and soared away for perpetual inspiration from the good; and by the will, which he calls faith, he won the realms of truth, beauty, and happiness. Such things can only be safely confided to the strong and pure-minded, and even they must isolate themselves in self-idolatry, and be "alone with the alone," and seek converse with the spirit of man's spirit.

But this prophet was educated by passion, and sought to be social with the weak; he therefore baptized spirituality in the waters of materialism. Instead of evolving the godlike nature of the human spirit, he endeavored to prove that humanity was already divinity, by investing Deity with what is manlike. Men were to be like gods by making gods men.

Various coincidences have occurred, which strikingly keep alive in the mountain brethren their idea of being the chosen of the Lord — and confirm them in the belief of the inspiration of the Book of Mormon. Among other things are the marks and hieroglyphical characters found engraved on the precipitous cliffs of southern Utah, which are faintly imitated by the present Indians. Those who were associated with Joseph as amanuenses pretend to have acquired sufficient knowledge of similar things to be enabled to decipher their signification, and have translated enough to confirm, in the most wonderful manner, the Nephite records.

The following is a specimen taken from the cliff in Sam Pete valley, at the city of Manti.

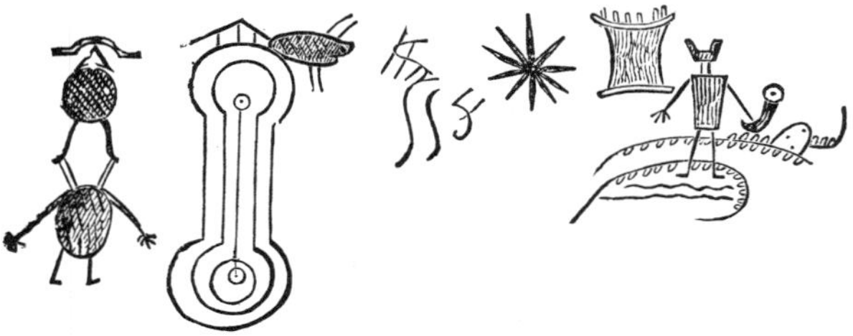

Translation by one of the Regents; "I Mahanti, the 2nd King of the Lamanites, in five valleys in the mountains, make this record in the 12 hundredth year since we came out of Jerusalem — And I have three sons gone to the South country to live by hunting antelope and deer."

Another specimen is taken from those in little Salt Lake Valley: they are reduced from three feet figures, preserving proportions.

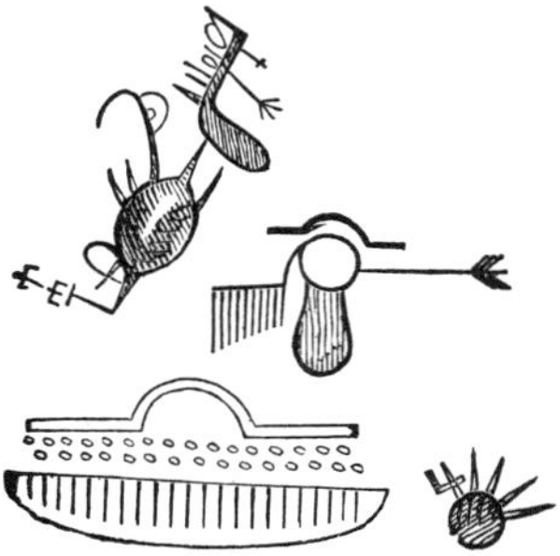

CHAPTER VI.

SOCIAL CONDITION OF THE MORMONS.

It may be reasonably expected that we should make some reference to the practical workings of this stupendous and complicated system on the present theatre of its application, in regard to their dealings with strangers and the state of morals among themselves.

During the sojourn of the party sent by the government to survey the region around the Great Lake, and ascertain its commercial and agricultural capabilities, the greatest kindness was shown to the members individually, and facilities given to prosecute the work. This was done, however, after it was ascertained that the advantages of the exploration would accrue to themselves, and that it was not for the purpose of seizing their lands, to bring them into market — the "let severely alone" policy was to have been adopted, if the character of the work had been to annoy them, which would have effectually paralyzed the operations.

A report that military men were coming to superintend a survey of their lands for the market, and interfere with their occupancy, had preceded the party. This occasioned it to be received with coldness, and among the more ignorant the prejudice was scarcely removed for the whole year. So that any interference with the triangulation stations, which was seldom, or any evasive answers to questions, were to be set down to ignorance more than to malice, and it is probable such a work could not have been conducted any where else with so little annoyance.

A large branch of the great emigration overland to California passed through the Mormon settlements, which is the best route across the country.

Of the parties organized in the States to cross the plains, there was hardly one that did not break into several fragments, and the division of property caused a great deal of difficulty. Many of these litigants applied to the courts of Deserêt for redress of grievances, and there was every appearance of impartiality and strict justice done to all parties. Of course, there would be dissatisfaction when the right was declared to belong to one side alone; and the losers circulated letters far and near, of the oppression of the Mormons. These would sometimes rebel against the equity decisions, and then they were made to feel the full majesty of the civil power. For contempt of court they were most severely fined, and in the end found it a losing game to indulge in vituperation of the court, or make remarks derogatory to the high functionaries.

Again, the fields in the valley are imperfectly fenced, and the emigrants' cattle often trespassed upon the crops. For this, a good remuneration was demanded, and the value being so enormously greater than in the States, it looked to the stranger as an imposition and injustice to ask so large a price. A protest would usually be made, the case then taken before the bishop, and the costs be added to the original demand. Such as these, were the instances of terrible oppression that have been industriously circulated as unjust acts of *heartless Mormons*, upon the gold emigration.

But provisions were sold at very reasonable prices, and their many deeds of charity to the sick and broken-down gold-seekers, all speak loudly in their favor, and must eventually redound to their praise. Such kindness, and apparently brotherly good-will among themselves, had its effect in converting more than one to their faith, and the proselytes deserted the search for golden ore, supposing they found there pearls of greater price.

Could the history of the overland emigrants, for the first two seasons after it commenced, be obtained and written, it would give us a volume of surpassing interest. Men thrown together and dependent on each other, would feel that very necessity of harmony an intolerable burthen, and selfishness, heartless and cruel, was developed to a frightful extent. There were instances

6*

of nobleness and good feeling, but the great mass of testimony goes to show much of the contrary.

There were many curious exercises of the feelings, and novel ways of proceeding. One sturdy German had well-nigh immortalized himself under the name of the "wheelbarrow man." His all was thus packed, and he trundled his wheelbarrow along as rapidly as the teams advanced, and had the prospect of reaching the end of his two thousand miles in safety. But alas! for the chances of human ambition—the Weber River in the mountains was swollen by the melting snows, and he was forced to cross on the raft with teams — the raft foundered in the swift current, and the wheelbarrow, with "his all," was swept down into the boiling kanyon below, and lost beyond redemption.

Resuming our theme, we may say that there were acts of individual churlishness, shown in the mountains, that call for reprobation, but they should not be charged upon the community; and, still more, it should not be thought that such actions were sanctioned by the chiefs of the people.

The homogeneousness of this sect consists in their obedience to counsel; but as the great majority is of course made up, like other communities, of all sorts of dispositions, they vary in habits and thinking according to individual character.

Thus they allow that mistakes have been made by individuals in carrying out their doctrines; for instance, many have supposed that the time was come when they should take possession of the property of the Gentiles, and that it would be no theft to secure cattle and grain from neighboring pastures and fields, thus "spoiling the Egyptians," and we are told by themselves that such conduct had to be forbidden from the public desk. This instance of wrong application of the dogma that they are "the stewards of the Lord, and the inheritance of the earth belongs to the saints," shows that some foundation exists for the charges against them, on the score of insecurity of property in Illinois and Missouri—and that abuses can easily arise from their principles, when residing near people of other religious views.

There is a casuistic view taken of the right to make a distinction between what is publicly proclaimed by the Seer, or under his approbation from the desk, and what may be called floating opinion, and practice also, arising from his private promulgations to certain members. On this they say that it is proper to deny certain things to exist *as doctrine*, which may be quite universally held and acted upon among them, because it has not been publicly proclaimed—and also to deny any thing offensive to the Christian world at large, especially when the affirmative would do others no good, and themselves harm; from which has arisen the opinion that they preach one thing abroad, and practise quite differently at home.

For to the initiated only is it given to know the "mysteries of the kingdom," and they hesitate not to rebuke the impertinent curiosity of the *Mormonish* at home, and the tares among the wheat — and meet the outsiders with a flat denial of what, to a true believer, would be readily admitted as correct. It is to them the pleading of guilty or not guilty of a court of justice.

Their casuistry makes this perfectly proper to their own minds, and it often turns on the meaning of certain words which convey a peculiar sense to each party. This can be made more plain by reference to the subject of "plurality of wives."

POLYGAMY.

It has been constantly denied that it is a doctrine of theirs to have "*spiritual* wives."

An intelligent lady informed me that she had considered it right, when asked by her friends, while on an eastern visit, to say that "it is no doctrine of ours to have spiritual wives;" and this, although the interrogators may have had in their minds nothing more than plurality and its supposed abuses.

That many have a large number of wives in Deserét, is perfectly manifest to any one residing long among them, and, indeed, the subject begins to be more openly discussed than formerly, and it is announced that a treatise is in preparation, to prove by the scriptures the right of plurality by all Christians, if not to declare their cwn practice of the same.

The revelation of Joseph on the subject of polygamy has probably never been printed, or publicly circulated. When he declared to the council the revelation, it was made known that he, like the saints of old, David, Solomon, and Jacob, and those He thought faithful, should be privileged to have as many wives as they could manage to take care of, to raise up a holy household for the service of the Lord. Immediately rumors were spread that the wives of many of the people were *re-married* to the leaders and high-priests, and subject to them, which they declared to be a slander; and maintain that the relation existing among them is a pure and holy one, and that their doctrine is, that every man shall have one wife, and every woman only one husband, as is laid down in the Book of Covenants by revelation.

Yet they affirm that this allows to the man a plurality, as the phrase is peculiarly worded; — the *only* applying to the female alone. They go so far as to say that our Savior had three wives, Mary and Martha and the other Mary whom Jesus loved, all married at the wedding in Cana of Galilee.*

Again, they teach that the use and foundation of matrimony is to raise up a peculiar, holy people for the Kingdom of God the Son, that at the Millennium they may be resurrected to reign with him, and the glory of the man will be in proportion to the size of his household of children, wives, and servants,—but that those

---

* Since writing the above, their teaching on this point is given by Orson Hyde, chief of the Apostles, in the Guardian of Dec. 26th, 1851. "If in Christ himself were fulfilled the words of Isaiah, 'He shall see his seed, he shall prolong his days, and the pleasure of the Lord shall prosper in his hand,' the Christian world are not mistaken in their opinion. But how were they fulfilled? If, at the marriage of Cana of Galilee, Jesus was the bridegroom and took unto him Mary, Martha, and the other Mary whom Jesus loved, it shocks not our nerves.

"If there were not an attachment and familiarity between our Savior and these women highly improper, only in the relation of husband and wife, then we have no sense of propriety, or of the characteristics of good and refined society. Wisely then was it concealed; but when the Savior poured out his soul unto death, when nailed to the cross, he saw his *seed of children*, but who shall declare his *generation?* No one,

eligible to the priesthood have only a right to marry at all.* It is to be a pure and holy state; and religious motives or a sense of duty, should alone guide; and that for sensual gratifications it is an abomination.

Infidelity and licentiousness are held up for abhorrence; and when the "plurality" law shall be promulgated, they will be punished by the decapitation of the offender and the severest chastity inculcated upon one sex, and rigid continence on the other during the gestation and nursing of children. Thus the time of weaning will again become a feast of joy, next to the celebration of the nuptial rite, and patriarchal times return.

Quoting the Scripture that "the man is not without the woman, nor the woman without the man," they affirm that it is the duty of every man to marry at least once, and that a woman cannot enter into the heavenly kingdoms without a husband to introduce her as belonging to himself.

And it has been said that some women, distrusting the title of their spouses to enter at all, have been desirous to take hold of the skirt of an apostle or high-priest with superior credentials; how far correct we are not sufficiently informed to state positively, and can only speak of such rumors as existing, and beg pardon for mentioning the scandal.

The addition of wives, after the first, to a man's family, is called a "sealing to him."

This constitutes a relation with all the rights and sanctions of

---

if he had *none* to be declared. Notwithstanding this, which to many is a new and strange feature in christianity, are we not disposed to mock at it, neither to regret salvation through the Virgin's son."

* On the 24th July last, the orator said: "Here let the sacred rights of matrimony, like the pure love of God 'spread undivided and operate unspent,' until the children of Abraham become as numerous as the stars above, or the sands below, that from the resurrection, the joint heirs of Jesus Christ may do the works that their Father did, till each in the centre of his own glory may reign in his own Eternity a God." "Let it be a sacred motto,—The woman that marries out of the priesthood, marries for hell."

matrimony;—and as they claim to have the only true priesthood, which alone can bind the parties in the holy state and make them "one flesh," it follows that they have the only true marriages now existing upon earth.

Thus guarded in the motive, and denounced as sin for other consideration than divine, the practical working of the system, so far as now extended, has every appearance of decorum. The romantic notion of a single love is derided, and met by calling attention to the case of parental affection; where the father's good will is bestowed alike on each of his many children; and they pretend to see a more rational application of a generous soul in loving more than one wife, than in the bigotry of a partial adhesion. The Seer alone has the power, which he can use by delegation, of granting the privilege of increasing the number of wives: the rule of primitive ages is applied in the case, and the suitor must first have the consent of the parents, then consult the lady, and the Seer.

Every unmarried woman has a right to demand a man in marriage, if she is neglected, on the ground of the privilege of salvation; and the President who receives the petition must provide for her; and he has the authority to command any man he deems competent to support her, "to seal her" to himself in marriage; and the man so ordered must show just cause and impediment why it should not be done, if he dislikes the union; or else be considered contumacious and "in danger of the council."

The Seer sometimes has to exercise his judgment in preventing incongruous sealings from unworthy motives, and to tell such that what they now esteem a privilege, will turn out soon to be a burden.

This interference with the kingdom of Cupid calls for most judicious measures on his part, for in that court his decisions, guided by Reason, are apt to be demurred to by Passion. But, as he can join, so too can he annul the contract, and dissolve the relationship of the parties, when, after he has counselled them and given them a proper probation, they still find an incompatibility to exist. Out of this matter grows an immense power, based upon his knowledge of all the domestic relations in the colony;—such delicate confidence begets a reverence and fear, and while things proceed harmoniously, a love to him as their adviser and friend. And as the peace of the society depends materially on that of families, he watches over this part of the prerogative with great solicitude, and keeps the parties, so far as practicable, up to their engagements.

In some instances several wives occupy the same house and the same room, as their dwellings have generally only one apartment, but it is usual to board out the extra ones, who most frequently "pay their own way," by sewing, and other female employments. It is but fairness to add that they hold the time near at hand pre dicted by Isaiah, "when seven women shall take hold of the skirt of one man and say, We will eat our own bread, but let us be called by thy name:"—which gives the assurance that plurality is foretold and correctly practised by them.

It is only a little in anticipation of the time when "the battles of the Lord" are to begin, and then, as the women are far more pure than the men, the females will greatly outnumber the males, for the latter will be swept off by sword and pestilence, and the other reserved to increase the retinue of the saints; and many women will thus be compelled to choose the same man, in order to secure a temporal home and temporal salvation, as also to obtain eternal right to a terrestrial or celestial queenship.

It is further maintained that there is great disparity of numbers between the sexes, and that the predominance of the female is more than can be accounted for from war, the dangers of the sea and other perils, and therefore nature indicates the propriety of plurality, as "marriage is honorable to all;" but the decision of this question can safely be intrusted to the relative numbers of the sexes, as exhibited in our census returns.

They also assure us that this system is the preventive and cure for the awful licentiousness—the moral and physical degradation in the world: and they make it both a religious and a social custom, a point of personal honour for a man whose wife, daughter, or sister has been led astray, to kill the seducer; and considering this as "common mountain law," based on the Mosaic code, a jury will acquit the murderer at all hazards.*

That the wives find the relation often a lonesome and burdensome one, is certain; though usually the surface of society wears a smiling countenance, and to all who consent from a sense of duty or enthusiasm the yoke is easy.

The wife of the prophet Joseph rebelled against it, and declared if he persisted she would desert for another, but the only satisfaction she received was "that a prophet must obey the Lord." When such wives rebel, the proceedings are very summary, and public opinion sustains the cause against the woman. A very exemplary lady in the valley is looked upon as having broken her vows for deserting the "Sealed one" and marrying another, and therefore is not invited into social parties.

An instance of summary proceeding came directly before us at Bear River. A Socialist emigrant from Monsieur Cabet'scommunity at Nauvoo, passed the winter at Salt Lake City, and in the spring started on his journey to California. He had in his train a woman with a child about two years old, who had applied to him for transportation to the land of gold, and represented that the dignitary to whom she had been "sealed" had not visited or provided for her for three years; and that a young man was betrothed to her who was in California, and if she could join him they should marry according to the laws of the land. The socialist's heart was touched, and he kindly offered her the means of proceeding, and they had come about one hundred miles when a posse overtook them, and demanded that the young woman should return to her legal or sealed husband. He consulted us whether to give up his charge — but the power precluded remonstrance, and the lady reluctantly retraced her steps.

* In the trial of Egan at Great Salt Lake City for killing, in cool blood the seducer of the wife, during the husband's absence, it was declared that civil damages marked the rottenness of other governments, and that "The principle, the only one that beats and throbs through the heart of the entire inhabitants of this territory, is simply this: *The man who seduces his neighbour's wife, must die, and her nearest relative must kill him.*"

Some other instances came under our notice, of like character, from which we must conclude that the regulation of the new "plurality" has not yet become perfect, and that the virtues claimed as pertaining to it are not in complete vigor; but we may add that the community had every appearance of good morals, so that any equal number of persons in the States can scarcely exhibit greater decorum.

Another method of increasing the household and adding to the glory of the chiefs is by "adoption." This consists in taking whole families and adopting them as part and parcel of the family of the chief, and arises out of the humility of the person so proposing to attach himself to the sacred character of some great dignitary of the church. There were pointed out to me, several who held this relationship to the Seers. The man is called, for instance, "Son of Brigham by adoption," and lives with him, or near by, and acts for him as a child does for his parent, and receives his subsistence, clothing, and living conjointly with the family.

This patriarchal stewardship method increases the authority of the presidency, and is intended to extend into the other world after the resurrection. It certainly speaks well for the kindness on the side of the patriarch, and for the belief in his holiness, and of truth in his teachings, in the estimation of those who attach themselves to the destinies of a fellow-man; while, at the same time, it shows how fanaticism can overcome the strongest feeling of independence.

Much has been said of the Mormon profanity, in the pulpit and out of it. But what is considered profanity by the world, is not thus considered with them—for they take their vain oaths without taking the name of the Supreme in connection with the words.

They curse or condemn with man's curses whenever they please, and such rough language sounds gratingly in refined ears, when it becomes usual in ordinary conversation — how they have learned to consider it innocent, we cannot imagine.

The using of the name of God is allowed only on judicial occasions, when a curse is laid upon some individual, as that of

Joseph upon Governor Boggs, who had one fulminated against him, accompanied by the prophecy that he should become a vagabond afflicted with a scab, and be loathsome to himself and all his former friends, wishing for death, without dying, for a long time.

When, therefore, we hear that their apostles and prophets have outraged decency in their temple language, let us bear in mind their education and instruction is to make a distinction between the most denunciatory words applied as expressions of dissent or emphasis, and taking the name of Jehovah in connection with the epithets, whereby they become blasphemy, and subject to severe civil penalty.

Like other new sects, they have their peculiar phraseology and terms of technical signification, which is "considered wisdom" in them; and, without knowing their import, a grievous misconception might be made.

Sometimes a ludicrous scene occurs in their meetings, arising from overwrought enthusiasm. One is related of a woman who sprang up and spoke "in tongues" as follows — "*Melai*, *Meli*, *Melee*," which was immediately translated into the vernacular by a waggish young man, who first observed that he felt "the gift of interpretation of tongues" sorely pressing upon him, and that she said in unknown words to herself, "my leg, my thigh, my knee." For this he was called before the council; but he stoutly persisted in his "interpretation" being by "the spirit," and they let him off with admonition.

In social parties and lively meetings the Mormons are preeminent, and their hospitality would be more readily extended to strangers, had they suitable dwellings to invite them into.

The adobe or sun-dried brick is now furnishing material, and the one-room log buildings are being replaced by spacious and commodious houses.

In their social gatherings and evening parties, patronized by the presence of the prophets and apostles, it is not unusual to open the ball by prayer, asking the blessing of God upon their amusements, as well as upon any other engagement — and then will follow the most sprightly dancing, in which all join with hearty good-will, from the highest dignitary to the humblest individual; and this exercise is to become part of the temple worship, to "praise God in songs and dances."

These private balls and soirées are frequently extended beyond the time of cock-crowing by the younger members, and the remains of the evening repast furnishes the breakfast for the jovial guests.

The cheerful, happy faces—the self-satisfied countenances—the cordial salutation of brother or sister on all occasions of address — the lively strains of music pouring forth from merry hearts in every domicil, as women and children sing their "songs of Zion," while plying the domestic tasks, give an impression of a happy society in the vales of Deserét.

The influence of their nomenclature of "brethren and sisters" is apparent in their actions, and creates the bond of affection among those who are more frequently thrown together. It is impressed on infantile minds by the constant repetition, and induces the feeling of family relationship. A little boy was asked the usual question, "whose son are you?" and he very naively replied, "I am brother Pack's son;" a small circumstance truly, but one that stamps the true mark of the Mormon society. The welfare of the order becomes therefore paramount to individual interest; and the union of hearts causes the hands to unite in all that pertains to the glory of the State; and hence we see growing up and prospering, the most enterprising people of the age — combining the advantages of communism, placed on the basis of religious duty and obedience to what they call the law of the gospel — transcending the notion of socialistic philosophers, that human regulations can improve and perfect society, irrespective of the revealed word and will of God.

Right or wrong, in the development of the principle and in its application, they have seized upon the most permanent element of the human mind in its social relations — not yielding fully to the doctrines of earnestness and universal intention, making man his own regenerator, as the fountain-head of truth, and passing thence into mysticism, pantheism, and atheism; neither endeavoring to cure the ills of society by political notions of trade and commerce, or by educating in the sentiment of honor, and by poetical inculcation of high thoughts and noble images, independent of being "born of the water and the spirit." We may use the words of one of their learned and most sincere men, to exhibit their view of obtaining the aggregate result of single efforts, which are these: "Our polity, I think, may be summed up in these few words — each person to operate at what and where he can do the best, and with all his might; being subject to the counsel of those above him."

To take that counsel is sometimes a bitter pill, and hundreds disobeyed it, and left sober earnings at home for the prospect of fortunes in the gold mines of California. The President and Council opposed emigration, though receiving abundance from the tithes by their superintendent there; and often declared that it would be a great calamity to discover mines in their own regions; for people would desert their farms and preparations for comfortable dwellings, for unsatisfying dross. Counsel on matrimonial matters is better obeyed. Bishop J—— was adding an apartment to a commodious house, and, having a small family, it caused a remark or question, why he thus extended his domicil. "Ah!" was the ready reply, "did you not know that he is obliged to take his brother's widow to wife, and the proper time is nearly arrived?" We remembered the case of the wife of seven brothers; and moreover, being only an humble layman, presumed not further to interrogate the acts of a bishop of that Melchisedek priesthood.

The subject of widows and widowers introduces some nice questions of rank and precedence in the future patriarchal courts. A lady of superior abilities and great enthusiasm, sealed later than the first wife, whose modest talents are thereby cast into the shade, may aspire to the place of first *queen*, TO BE: and thus an affectionate rivalry can be raised, of which the expectant king reaps the sole benefit. The widow of several husbands must have doubts to which she shall owe her elevation, unless she fortunately loved one supremely — and the wife finds a rival in the brother's widow, from the tie of consanguinity. The troubles of the high Chieftain are said to arise from still another cause.

He had a wife dearly beloved before becoming a Mormon, who died out of his church; but she can be saved by substituted baptism, and his next partner has become exceedingly anxious to know whether her predecessor will be resurrected to be the chief of the queens, or if that important station is reserved for herself, who has partaken of so "much tribulation." Why the question is not categorically answered we cannot opine—but, if women ever *do* teaze, we may suppose such a subject likely to call out all their resources to gratify curiosity.

CHAPTER VII.

THE PRIESTHOOD, SCHOOLS, ETC.

THE powers of the priesthood are thus stated in the Guardian; the "gift of faith, discerning of spirits, prophecy, revelation, visions, healing, tongues, and the interpretation of tongues, wisdom, charity, brotherly love." Pre-eminent in all these is the head man of the priestly order; supposed to be, and looked up to as, the Lord's peculiar prophet, with ability to read the hearts of men, his spiritual authority is complete; and having so large a share of the wealth of the people at his command, and their entire will submissive to his behests, the President of the Latter-Day Saints is the most autocratic ruler in the world. But his great authority has thus far been made subservient to the public interests, and his attention never diverted from alleviating individual distress — therefore it is no wonder that his sanctity is believed above reproach, and his least wish abjectly complied with by almost all over whom he presides with unlimited sway.

Yet it is more the office than the man that carries such a prestige of command with those intimately connected with the source of power, or with the mass at a distance—there is not the usual man-worship found in the admirers of splendid abilities and achievements of the founders of religious sects. The people are mostly composed of those converted in foreign lands, whose necks have been bent to force, instead of yielding obedience by choice; and their present condition is one of greater freedom and elevation of character than while groaning under civil despotism. Taught to regard themselves as the chosen of the Lord, soon to act on a theatre of renown and glory, with angels and saints to look on, and cheer them with celestial applause for noble deeds, they cheerfully await the signal of heaven to march under its banner;

and they lend their means to bring up to their rendezvous all who will fraternize with them, and listen to the voice of their shepherd, wherever wandering in the wastes of the moral world, and so soon as its tones are heard, gladly turn to the green pastures of truth in the mountains, and come out to strengthen the cords of the "Stake of Zion."

A cardinal point being an unshaken belief in the inspiration of Joseph the Seer, and that the prophetic mantle has fallen on his successor Brigham, the new church Elijah and Elisha; any reflections derogatory to the character of either, based on suspicion, innuendo, or hearsay, is an insult of the darkest dye to them. But this adoration is not universal; nor must we look upon all as ignorant and blindfolded, guided along the ditch of enthusiasm by self-deluded leaders. Indeed, almost every man is a priest, or eligible to the office, and ready armed for the controversial warfare; his creed is his idol; and while among the best proselyters we class many that are least versed in literary attainments, still, among them we find liberally educated men, and those who have been ministers in other denominations — in fact there seems to be as fair a sample of intelligence, moral probity, and good citizenship, as can be found in any nominal Christian community.

Sincerity and simplicity of purpose mark the masses, which virtues have been amply proved by the sacrifices and sufferings endured. And among that people, so submissive to counsel, are those who watch with eagle eye that first principles are adhered to, and stand ready to proclaim apostacy in chief or in layman; and scrutinizing all revelations to discover whether they are from the Lord, or given through his permission by Satan, to test the fidelity and watchfulness of the disciples of truth.

It was in conformity with this watchful and scrutinizing spirit on the part of those determined to adhere strictly to first principles, that the volumes presented by Gladden Bishop, the revelations of Rigdon and others, were pronounced to have a demon character; and the pretensions of William Smith and J. J. Strang, the Beaver Island "King," declared to be spurious, and they, with their followers, were solemnly excommunicated.

EDUCATION.

In Utah or Deserét, the arrangements for the cause of education are upon an extensive scale.

Hitherto all exertion has necessarily been bestowed on obtaining the means of living; to fence fields, build houses, and tend their crops and herds. But as soon as this pressure slackened, we find them appropriating liberally for a university, which shall be eminently practical in its character, and designed to teach the useful branches thoroughly, first, to all, and allow those who have the leisure and the means, to acquire the ornamental afterwards.

The selected grounds for the university buildings are beautifully located on the first broad terrace, in the north part of the temple city, and overlook the dwellings of the town. City Creek has excavated a deep channel through this table-land, as it bursts out from the mountains, and its waters are to be taken at the requisite elevation in the hills, and conducted to the college plat, and made to beautify the scenery in jets, and water the groves, walks, and botanical gardens; and a part used for health, in extensive bath and swimming houses.

A large square is to be allotted and fitted to athletic and equestrian exercises; an observatory for practical astronomy, and the instruments already collected are to be freely used to instruct on the ground, in the several departments of engineering, mechanics, and surveying—the agricultural department liberally patronised; and the living, spoken languages of all peoples thoroughly taught to the proper students.

A peculiar feature in their instruction is the introduction of a "Parent's school" for the heads of families; and, at the time of the organization, the President is said to have avowed his intention of attending it as a scholar, which is gladly mentioned as a thing redounding to his praise, and showing his strength of character; as also calculated to show others of his people that the time for acquiring knowledge is during the whole life of man. It is too often that the school-room is deserted in early life, or the idea acted upon, that, if our youthful days have not acquired the elementary branches, it is of no use afterwards to try to remedy the deficiency.

The Parents' school, patronized by the Presidency and Regents of the University, with the members of the High Council, must have an immense influence in refining, elevating, and ennobling the mind of the public generally. Primary schools, opened under the direction of the chancellor, and inspected by the Regents, are well attended by the children; but the whole system is now like chaos being reduced to order. Their philosophers already aspire to something more than has yet been accomplished; and they assert that they shall soon revolutionize the kingdom of science, and surpass the most learned in mathematics, philosophy, and the sciences of observation.

The geologist and chemist must directly come to them to learn the wonders developed from below, and in the mineral kingdoms; and the botanist and naturalist to study the arcana of the principle of life, elaborated in the vegetable and animal. For, having "sought first the kingdom of Heaven," they look now for the promise of having all other things and knowledge added; but they sensibly add, that the Lord helps those who help themselves, and that their minds will only be quickened to perceive by the most intense industry.*

---

* From one of the Regents, speaking of the University. — Phelps' 24th July Oration, 1851. — "Beseeching the whole church to pray the Lord, our Heavenly Father, to send down some of the Regents from the great University of Perfection, as he did to Noah, Moses, and others, to unfold unto his servants the principles of wisdom, philosophy, and science, which are truth."—"But what with all the precious things of time, the inventions of man, the records from Japhet in the ark to Jonathan in Congress, embracing the wit and the gist, the fashions and the folly, which so methodically, grammatically, and transcendantally grace the libraries of the elite of nations, really be worth to a saint, when our Father sends down his regents, the angels, from the grand library of Zion above, with a copy of the *History of Eternal Lives;* the records of worlds; the *Genealogy of the Gods;* the philosophy of truth; the *names of our spirits* from the Lamb's Book of Life; and the songs of the sanctified?"— It must be recollected that things on earth are but patterns of those in the celestial planet, according to Mormonism.

The greatest change will be made in astronomy—the system of the world will be modified in the number, arrangement, and relations of the planets; and any curious to anticipate what is to burst upon us, may discover an inkling in the Book of Abraham, which was brought to Nauvoo with some Egyptian mummies; of which Joseph translated a portion written by the faithful patriarch, when he sojourned on the banks of the Nile, which relates to the planetary world; diving to the centre of the universe, and exhibiting the great orb Kolob, which revolves on its axis once in a thousand of our years, and around which all else that relates to man is supposed to wheel in endless lines.

Their most profound mathematician, while in England, put forth a *feeler* essay, by which the Newtonian theories of gravitation, attraction, and repulsion, are overthrown; and all the effects usually attributed to them put upon the intelligence of element; and the motions of the universal atoms, either single or combined in mass, referred to the circumscribing and infusing power and presence of the Holy Spirit, acting directly upon, and through all things. We have not time and perhaps patience would fail to follow the data and the argument used to prove this,—and we may safely trust all developments of this kind to their practical hands, and rely upon experiment to furnish them with facts that shall bring them into physical truth; and hope that their researches will contribute something to the cause of science, and that their admirable theory of education, when fully carried out, will aid and enrich our literary treasures.

It is understood that the Saxon and Celtic classics, from which four-fifths of our spoken words are derived, will have a prominent place and comparative attention, and stand side by side in barbaric native strength with the more polished Greek and Latin. The sciences of observation, just taking a perfect form, and which meet more nearly the demand of the age in the educational market; which are spread before the eye of every one that walks the field, tills the ground, or observes nature's curious ways in the house, the shop, the study, or under open skies, are those that will be pursued with the greatest ardor.

By the liberality of the last Congress, the delegate from Utah was furnished the means to select a fine library, and this munificence will greatly aid the cause of education at their Zion University. "To search for wisdom in all good books" was the behest of their great prophet, and the sentiment is fully inculcated on all.

This people are jealous of their rights, and feel themselves entitled to enforce order by their own laws, and severely punish contempt of them.

The administration of justice is of the most simple kind, and based on equity and the merits of the question, without reference to the precedents and technicalities, referring to the rules of the Mosaic code, and its manner of punishment, when applicable.

Witnesses are seldom put on oath in the lower courts, and there is nothing known of the "law's delay," and the quibbles whereby the ends of truth and justice may be defeated. But they have a criminal code called "The Laws of The Lord;" which has been given by revelation, and not yet promulgated; the people not being able quite to bear it, or the organization still too imperfect. It is to be put in force, however, before long, and when in vogue, all grave crimes will be punished and atoned for, by cutting off the head of the offender. This regulation arises from the fact, that "without shedding of blood there is no remission"—and is intended as an act of mercy to the criminal, who, when he has unwisely or through Satanic wiles, jeoparded his salvation by evil acts, can, by willingly offering his neck to the block, atone for all his sins, and enter on the "untried state of being" absolved from guilt, through the sacrifice of his own blood, and obedience to this "law of the Lord."

LOYALTY.

Though this people fled to a foreign country to enjoy the liberty that persecution denied them in the states, as soon as they found their adopted land had come under the jurisdiction of the stripes and stars—which their own valor had helped to win in the army of the Pacific against Mexico,—they embraced the earliest opportunity of declaring their adherence to the great charter of liberty and national glory, and announced to the world that it was given to our patriot fathers by divine inspiration, and that they will uphold and defend it, though all the original parties shall secede and trample it under foot.

"They will make no law forbidden by the *sacred* constitution of the United States," and predict that the day is not far distant when they shall be solicited by patriotic American citizens, to descend from their rocky fastnesses, to enforce its sanctions upon those led astray by frantic political delusion and anarchy.

The great "eagle of America is now perched on her mountain eyrie, watching the unsafe wanderings of her brood; and, ready to stretch her pinions for the flight, will soon collect them together again, and bear them on her wings to a place of safety." Firmly cherishing the belief of their divine mission to revolutionize the world, and that events are even now shaped to expedite their return to the promised land Zion, they note the crimes, the follies and turmoils in every place, and a record of them is kept and filed away with the archives of their church and state. These are held up as portents to demonstrate that the wrath of heaven is already being poured out, and the madness of political factions, the bitter strifes of different religions,—the wars of nations, and of peoples against their governments, together with the ravages of the cholera plague, all are declared to show the beginning of the end, and to herald the ultimate triumph of Mormonism.

The books they keep are to be some of those at the great judgment, when "the books are opened"—their prophet has told them to keep a faithful record; and their scribes are busy in forwarding the awful accounts that shall condemn this generation.

They enter into the dark alleys of crowded cities, and ferret out the practices of secret associations in the dens of pollution; and the details equal all the imagination can picture of the sins of Sodom and Gomorrha. They note down the aberrations from rectitude of the men entrusted with making and executing our laws, or who minister at the altars of divine worship in this and other countries, until their criminal calendar of nations smells rank to heaven, and causes their members to regard themselves, in point of purity, in comparison, as clothed with the resplendent white robe of righteousness.

And the listener to the eulogiums of Mormonism is pointed to the success that has attended their efforts — and they proudly challenge him to parallel the fact, that, without "scrip or purse," an obscure individual, in the open light of the age which should be styled the most intelligent, from having the accumulated knowledge of those gone before to add to its own wisdom, should set on foot a scheme by which the deep mystery of a continent, peopled by two different races, is solved; the one swept off ere history began their record, save on the broken column and fallen arches of crumbling granite; the other without tradition of its origin, fast following its predecessor to oblivion, but now taught how to redeem its remnant, and knowing whence it came, regain pristine favor with heaven, in the path of duty well marked out—and which, in twenty years, has multiplied its devotees from six individuals to three hundred thousand—founded a state in the far off wilderness, and compelled a mighty nation to recognise them a separate people, with the right of self-government—proclaimed its mission on all the grand divisions of the earth, and taken converts from the patriarchal states of Rome, and the pagan isles of the ocean; all this, too, while the fiercest persecution was chasing them from one refuge to another, and, under the ban of obloquy, impeaching their motives and the purity of their lives, as well as the scope of their doctrines.

But what we predicate of their teachings and of their doctrines to-day, may not be the truth of either to-morrow. For by the doctrine of development, and having revelations according with the exigencies of the church, they may be bidden to change their policy, and suspend those commands found to be inapplicable to their condition, and the *faith* of the saints.

Such suspension and withdrawal of privileges have already become precedents — and it should not strike us with surprise to hear that matrimony is confined again to a single pair, on the plea that it has fulfilled the intention of its founder, and the word is prevailing fast enough to built up the faith on the earth, ready for the Lord's coming.

The present Seer has cautioned his people to be faithful, and they may hope any hour to receive a deputation from the "lost ten tribes of Israel," which shall confirm them, and signal the conversion of their red brethren, when "a nation shall be born in a day." These lost tribes are supposed to be on a fragmentary part of the earth, which is either in space revolving with its parent planet, and called, as it is placed there "The North Country," or on some insular land, to which no vessel has ever been permitted to sail and return to publish the place of abode. And there are four witnesses to the truth of the Gospel who have never tasted death; these are, St. John the Evangelist, who was to tarry till the Lord came, if he so willed it; and three others of the church founded in America by Christ, who begged the like privilege and had it granted to them, as may be seen by consulting the Book of Mormon.

These saints continue in perpetual manhood, and travel over the earth, assuming the language and costume of the country they happen to be in, and have visited some of the brethren of the Latter-Day Church, according to their own belief in receiving some remarkable strangers: they look anxiously for their appearance, to proclaim boldly their character and instruct the *people* from the temple pulpit; but this too will depend upon *their* faithful obedience to spiritual ***counsel.***

The Lord will not come till the Temple of Reception is built; the temple will rise only by the efforts of a people *specially* organized in the faith; and this generation may fail and be rejected, but another may be raised up to do the work appointed, who will obey the revelation; so is it taught and written.

Thus have we endeavored to draw a true picture of the mountain Mormons; — the view was taken before ever seeing any history of their doctrines or polity by others; — it is the result of observation and listening to their teachings, and reading a few of their own accredited books; and, as far as possible, we have endeavored to make them sketch their own portrait.

The policy of our own government in giving them rulers selected from themselves, is so just to them in their present condition, and so well calculated to allay their irritated feelings, aroused by the injustice and oppression of the mobs, which were left unrebuked if not sanctioned by state authorities, that it cannot be too much commended.

It has caused a revulsion of feeling, and taught them to make a distinction between the lawless acts of congregated individuals, and the governors of the state, and the sense of gratitude and kindness is shown by their lately selecting a site for a city in the beautiful Parvan valley, in the county of *Millard*, to be called *Fillmore*, which shall be the civil Capital of the territory, as the Temple City is the head quarters and Capital for the higher spiritual power. The magnanimity of a people, far separated from all others, is thus appealed to, instead of wounding their pride,—it is the field on which the freedom of conscience is to be tried;—it is the cause of political liberty, successfully contended for by the revolutionary fathers, in the estimation of that portion of American citizens; and under the permanent law of Congress, they ask for self-government to test their fealty as a matter of right and justice.

Therefore, we may be permitted to say, that this course of judicious action may secure a law-abiding people; and soon we may expect to see a thriving, peaceful state added to the extending Union under the name of Deserét — The Land of the Honey Bee.

PART SECOND.—HISTORY.

CHAPTER I.

EARLY PERIOD OF MORMONISM.

In what has preceded, we have aimed more to give a view of the people of Utah, the Mormons, as they delineate themselves, than to criticise their creed, or controvert their pretensions. During a year's residence among them, there was an opportunity of observing them impartially, and having no knowledge of their doctrines in advance, their whole system became one of study, unfettered by prejudice. Since leaving them, curiosity has led me to investigate the motives of the opposition which they have encountered, both in regard to their religious opinions and political actions.

We find that they are regarded by many as dangerous to the state, and subverters of our holy religion. The system is held up as the result of impudent imposture, and interested knavery. Their miracles, which had so much to do in its early success, are accounted for in the same manner as those of the Mesmeric philosopher, or those of a monkish priesthood:—the performers of them perhaps deceived themselves and the lookers-on, duped by a deceiving imagination, and led astray by a deluding superstition. They call up historical facts, and exhibit before us similar fanaticism in all ages of the church, in which whole countries and communities have been overwhelmed for a time, and which passing away, are the wonder of after ages; and we come to the melancholy conclusion that nothing is too absurd when it assumes the name of religion, to have its thousands of votaries.

By this rule of historical evidence,—by the facts contemporaneous with the development of Mormonism, are we called upon to test the truth of its origin in heavenly revelation or successful human derivation.

The addition to the Sacred Record, The Book of Mormon, is at the foundation of the scheme, and we will first see how it is proved to be the work of one of sufficient genius to produce it; and then show how it has been made to lay so firm a hold on many minds. Its style and literary merits are not parts of the question at all — we have only to observe that it is the most successful attempt ever made to imitate the Scriptures, not in its composition, but in its pretension to be an inspired text.

There have been several versions of the story, but, after the most mature investigation we have been enabled to give to the subject, the following seems most consistent with the facts yet published. All is established on the most positive testimony of individuals under oath, which is essential to the point at issue. As this will controvert the statements of the "Prophet," Joseph Smith, and his father's family, we ask the opinion of their neighbors whether their assertions are entitled to unquestioned credit. Fifty-one gentlemen of Palmyra, New York, and eleven of Manchester, and several persons who lived near the family residence, and often labored for days in company with them, all testify to the same effect —"that they consider them destitute of that moral character, which ought to entitle them to the confidence of any community — and particularly that the senior and junior Josephs, were entirely unworthy of belief in such matters; and addicted to vicious habits." They were visionary men, and believed that hidden treasures were in the vicinity, and often employed themselves in digging for them and money. They used what in Scotland are denominated "Seer-stones," through which persons, born under peculiar circumstances, can see things at a distance, or future events passing before their eyes, or things buried in the earth.* Such a stone was dug from a well by one Willard Chase, which was loaned to the prophet Joseph, and retained by him, and with which some of the family declared he read in the Golden Bible.

* Like the Mediæval Crystallomancy.

In after times, he said that he used two stones, set in the two rims of a bow, the Urim and Thummim of the ancients; and probably this seer-stone gave rise to the idea that it would be a sure way of gaining belief. These stones are those spoken of in the Book of Mormon, as the ones touched by the finger of God for the use of Jared in his barges, when he crossed the Pacific to settle America. They became shining lights in his dark vessel. The family also used peach and witch-hazel rods, to detect and drive off evil spirits, when digging for money; and such branches are supposed by many to point out streams of running water beneath the surface; and are used by miners frequently to find the lodes of mineral, for the currents of water are presumed to run parallel with the veins. They take a forked stick, and hold a prong in each hand, the stem pointing upward, and walk about the field; — if there are any underground springs, the stick will turn downward toward it in spite of the holder. Tales of such discoveries are told among this people, and firmly believed at present, not alone by them, but by persons in every part of the country.

It has already been mentioned that in 1823, under the preaching of a Methodist elder, the "prophet," as we shall continue to call Joseph, and his father's family, were converted or excited, in a "revival of religion." This resulted in giving a portion to the Presbyterians, but leaving the prophet greatly perplexed among the rival sects, who were striving to enlist the converts under some particular banner. In viewing "this struggle for the spoils of victory," his original mind took the idea that there was but little to choose between them, and that all matters wrangled upon were mere opinions. Yet he could see that there was a religious element in the human character, which was apt to be swayed by the circumstances surrounding the individual. On that little theatre were shown the scenes attending the preaching of Peter the Hermit, the enthusiasm of the disciples of Matthias of Munster, on a diminished scale; but enough to exhibit the tendency of fanaticism and mystic feeling in a multitude. And he did not fail to observe that a permanent influence remained when the exciting causes were over — that some would continue their course, and search out reasons to substantiate their notions, instead of testing them in cool judgment, their pride or their vanity being enlisted—others, feeling a depression of spirits, would unite in social gatherings and rouse what they called "a happy feeling," by harangues and vociferous prayers—and not a few would join in the popular current to be with their friends, and enjoy variety and novelty.

During this rivalry of the sects, also, their peculiar views were freely discussed, of course, and to one so observant, their theological notions, supported each by Bible Commentaries, were well digested by Joseph. Could a compounded system be deduced from them that would suit a majority of minds, and their attention joined to it, the task of founding a "new church," would not seem a very great work to one who looked upon each of those bodies bearing the name, as equally a true one, or only organizations for carrying out human purposes. Judging from what he says in his autobiography, ideas of this kind now took possession of his mind, on which he systematically acted during the remainder of his career. He informs us that he engaged in earnest prayer for enlightenment. He rose at night and continued his supplications. In September of that year, when all else was hushed in sleep, his prayers were answered by a heavenly vision. An angel in all the splendor of light, radiating from his head, with eyes of lambent flame, and hair like fleecy wool, stood before him. His message was that Joseph should gird himself for the work of the Lord, and go forth among men and restore His church. No doubt he had a remarkable dream that night, waking or sleeping—for though the vision was repeated in the most resplendent manner, and important revelations given concerning the manner of founding a "new church," and information upon the subject of hidden records on plates of gold in the vicinity—yet he informs us that he "went about his work as usual on the following morning." The conception of the plan might well be called his "brilliant glory:" in figurative language original thoughts are visiting angels, and mature reflections heavenly counsellors. There was a floating story abroad that a golden Bible had been found in Canada, and many little circumstances conspired soon, to give consistency to what was then planned for a future development.

About this period Joseph leaves his father's residence, and for four years was passing to and fro between Wayne, New York, and Susquehanna counties, Pennsylvania. The first two years are much involved in mystery; the autobiography helps us to little knowledge of the manner in which they were passed on the line of travels and sojourns in the counties of Onondaga and Chenango, though it is asserted that his name can be found on the criminal records, having been arrested as a vagabond. He acquired great reputation for money-digging. A man by the name of Stowell, in Bainbridge, New York, employed him to dig for hidden treasure in the neighborhood. Some legends of the wandering Spaniards from De Soto's band, and the wealth of the aboriginal inhabitants buried on the banks of the Susquehanna, had fired the imaginations of the old Dutchman, and a company was in search of the untold wealth. The seer-stone and the mineral rod were already familiar to Joseph, and his pretensions and frequent search caused him to be called the "money-digger."

While laboring in his profession at Harmony, Pennsylvania, he became acquainted with Miss Hale, and persuaded her to elope with him, and they were clandestinely married. Previous to this, however, he had made a journey home, and there reported that silver ore was to be had on the Susquehanna, and induced one Laurence to carry him back, promising to share with him in an enterprise to fill a boat with ore, and carry it to Philadelphia. On searching for the mine, it could not be found, and the man went back disappointed. In 1826, Joseph again duped his friend Stowell, by telling him that he had discovered, near his father's residence, a bar of gold in a cave, and offered to go and cut it off with a chisel, and give him one half of it, if Stowell would move him and wife to Wayne County. Though all former trials had failed, the honest old fellow consented, and with his stout team carried him back; but then Joseph refused to leave his bride among strangers, and the Dutchman returned to his home to cultivate his cabbages, and to regret once more the "golden opportunity" lost. This is the substance of the history of the time between the first angelic apparition and the announcement that the plates had been delivered him by the angel, and the translation begun.

The whole explication of the Book of Mormon hangs on the satisfactory solution of a few obscure points in the following circumstances. A Romance to show the manner of peopling America by some Jews and the "lost ten tribes of Israel;" the wars, and economy of living among their descendants, and the division into tribes as they were found in our Indians at the discovery by Columbus, is known to have been written by the late Rev. Mr. Spalding at Conneaut, Ohio. This was just previous to 1812, and his brother testifies that their "arts, sciences and civilization were brought into view, in order to account for all the curious antiquities found in various parts of North and South America." A clear idea of the work can be had from the affidavit of Mr. Henry Lake, given at Conneaut, in 1833, which is corroborated by abundant other testimony.

He affirms: "I left the state of New York in the year of 1810, and arrived in this place about the first of January following. Soon after my arrival I formed a copartnership with Solomon Spalding * * *. He frequently read to me from a manuscript which he was writing, and which he entitled the "Manuscript Found," which he represented as being found in this town. I spent many hours in hearing him read said writings; and became acquainted with their contents. He wished me to assist him in getting it printed, alleging that a book of that kind would meet with a rapid sale. This book represented the American Indians as the lost tribes, gave an account of their leaving Jerusalem, their contentions and wars, which were many and great. One time, when he was reading to me the tragic account of Laban, I pointed out to him what I considered an inconsistency, which he promised to correct; but by referring to the Book of Mormon, I find to my surprise it stands there, just as he read it to me then. Some months ago I borrowed a golden Bible, * * * had not read twenty minutes before I was astonished to find the same passages in it that Spalding had read to me, more than twenty years before, from his "Manuscript Found." Since then, I have more fully examined the said golden bible, and have no hesitation in saying that the historical part of it is principally, if not wholly, taken from the "Manuscript Found." I well recollect telling Mr. Spalding that the too frequent use of the words, "Now it came to pass," "And it came to pass," rendered it ridiculous. Spalding left here in 1812, and I furnished him with the means to carry him to Pittsburg, where he said he would get the book printed and pay me. But I never heard any thing more from him, or of his writings, till I saw them in the Book of Mormon."

The same in effect is the evidence of the brother of Spalding, that he heard much of the "Manuscript" read, and that, according to his best recollection, "The Book of Mormon is the same as my brother Solomon wrote, with the exception of the religious matter." All this is confirmed by more than half a dozen other gentlemen, and by the widow and daughter of the author of "Manuscript Found." It was also made known that a change in his original design was made. At first the Romance began, by fitting out the emigrant Jews at Rome, and a quire of paper was written; — but not liking that origin, he started from Jerusalem, with Lehi and his four sons, as the leaders of the enterprise, under divine instruction.

We have followed the Manuscript Found to Pittsburg; its further traces are not so palpable. It has been supposed it was left with the printer Lambdin, and that Sidney Rigdon was employed to edit it for the press; and that, by collusion with Smith, whose money-digging reputation was notorious, the miraculous plan of translation was concerted. Subsequent events discredit this supposition. The author of the Manuscript left Pittsburg in 1814, and two years afterwards died in the southern part of Pennsylvania. His widow, shortly after this event, removed to Onondaga county, New York, near to her early residence, and carried a trunk thither, containing the writings of her deceased husband. She spent much of her time for three years in visiting her friends in adjoining counties, and resided awhile at Hartwick, not far from the home of the Stowell above mentioned. During a part of the time from 1817 to 1820, when she again married and moved to Massachusetts, the trunk, supposed to contain the writings, was at her brother's in Onondaga Hollow, near the residence of the Smith family; — Wayne and Onondaga counties being separated by a narrow township of land.

When the Book of Mormon appeared, and its almost identity with the Manuscript was discovered by those familiar with the latter, enquiry was made for the whereabouts of that paper. It had mysteriously disappeared, and the "Manuscript Found" has ever since been the Manuscript lost. The trunk was hunted up and searched, but only the quire of paper with the Roman exodus was in it; out of all that it formerly contained, this alone was left. How the Manuscript could have been taken out, and when, remains a mystery, and probably ever will remain unknown. Like the history of the first Mormon Seer, the transits of that trunk can hardly now be traced in those same counties of Chenango, Otsego, and Onondaga,—and what process was going on in the interiors of each, is left to conjecture. But a curious coincidence of dates and habitations exists between them, which subsequent developments connect together.

From these circumstances, just hinted at in the above account, it seems fair to conclude, that the Manuscript Found escaped from its prison and perched upon some farmer's shelf; or fell direct, by accident or design, into the hands of Joseph Smith, and opportunely met the mind that could mould it into a religious fiction. Much has been said of his stupidity and illiterate character; but no doubt these qualities, if a negation may be so denominated, are greatly exaggerated. Like the cobbler at his Pilgrim's Progress, people took the profession and scholastic lore of the man as the measure of his genius. But what is genius? and who will venture to define it? Its effects we see, and turn aside from the humdrum of life to observe how it rivets the attention of many to its artistic creations, and whirls them out of the eddies of their own thoughts and opinions into the onward current,—to think and believe in those of the author.

Here is a book that takes fast hold of the minds of hundreds of thousands, and so skilfully arranged on the model of the true Bible, and so garnished with versions and extracts of its text, that it becomes to them a verisimilitude of the Holy Book itself. Such wonderful influence is not due to those extracts alone, which constitute one eighteenth part of the whole; but rather to the ingenious arrangement of its plot, and the decided non-committalism to any sect of Christians or prominent doctrine; if we except the mode of administering the rite of baptism in the Nephite churches.

Nor was that a stupid man who could wield the powers of life and death over a multitude in an enlightened age and community, and cause his memory to be revered by the sincere, and gain in their estimation the proud position of being "the most perfect man and powerful mind we ever saw;" for such an eulogium have we often heard.

He had a religious turn of mind, and at the "great revival" an impression was surely made, the stamp of which was never effaced from his character. He emerged from the conflicting waves of various religious opinions and visionary speculations raging around him; and sought to arrange a system that would suit all minds, and draw them into one communion. His associations were vulgar, but such as made him acquainted with the weak side of humanity. He early saw that numbers were of more consequence than intellectual attainments in the sects, in point of influence. It is a prime point to enlist the less cultivated many, which at last invariably carries the unstable part of the cultivated few; who, if they do not yield a full acquiescence, are willing to be reckoned of the host, and think to lead by non-resistance.

The first idea must have been to make a book that should account for the peopling of America, and the ruins that are spread over much of its surface, showing evidences of a former civilization. Various theories were afloat on this mysterious subject. That of Jewish origin is an old one. The traditions collected from the Indians and compared with the Asiatic — the disappearance of the ten tribes, and Hebrew notions among the aborigines — the discovery of ruined cities and temples in Central

America — the relics of pottery, bricks, and stumps of axe-cut trees, buried far beneath the surface of the Mississippi valley—all had conspired to arouse curiosity. The book that should gain the credit of elucidating these subjects would be highly remunerative.

But some slight incidents occurring while such thoughts were revolving in his mind, gave a further and wider grasp to the plan. The biblical language of the manuscript, and the report then abroad that a gold Bible had been dug up in Canada, suggested the idea of calling it a Bible. In crossing a swampy grove, he found some pure white sand one day, left by a retiring freshet; and he wrapped up a specimen in his frock, and carried it home. The family were at dinner. He announced to them that he had found a gold Bible. They seemed to believe him, and asked to see it. He gravely said that the angel forbade, for the person who should look upon it without authority should die. He was credited, and a few days after told a neighbor that he "had fixed the fools, and would have some fun." By this he saw the family were ready for any imposture.

The plan being laid, and the manuscript in his possession in some way that he did not fear detection, he must then have determined to alter it to suit his own conceptions, from which a golden harvest was anticipated. It must have been with him, and secreted at the first visit to his father's house in 1826; for, at that time, all of them set various rumors afloat, and very contradictory ones indeed, about a book found in the ground—and the complete history of its supernatural origin was not given until after its publication. The lucky accidents might well be considered by him as his providences, and the kindness of a good angel.

The next attempt was on the credulity of Martin Harris, a miserly, visionary man, who had been a member successively of several denominations. Meeting him, he abruptly told him that the Lord had commanded him to advance fifty dollars to begin the work of translation, and represented the great rewards to follow. Harris's cupidity gave credit, if his judgment of the divine mission was staggered. With this money the last visit to Harmony was made, and on his return the work commenced, and

Harris became the scribe for a few weeks; and like Baruch for Jeremiah, "he wrote the words as he pronounced them with his mouth." Harris became fully committed, furnished the means of publication, by which he was pecuniarily ruined, preached the doctrine three years, and finally deserted what to him was a foundered ark. Harris was shortly substituted by a better scholar, Oliver Cowdery, a schoolmaster, who wrote out the five hundred octavo pages, and became one of the witnesses to its divine origin, though he too failed and dissented in after times.

The manner of writing was as follows: Smith would place his pseudo gold plates in a hat, and take the stones, Urim and Thummim, which he affirmed had been delivered to him at the hill Cumora, in Palmyra, by an angel—and, raising a screen of cloth between himself and the scribe, proceed to look through the stones, and the words, in reformed Egyptian characters, would change to his vernacular, and "pass before his eyes by the power and gift of God." He either concealed portions of the manuscript, or committed them to memory before beginning the day's work, and thus dictated to his amanuensis.

He gives us a graphic account of the first persecution by his neighbors, who tried to capture the "gold plates"—and to escape from this, he concealed them in a barrel of beans and started for Pennsylvania again. A writ for debt was served on him under a pretence, and he was overtaken and searched by the sheriff, but the functionary of the law was not bright enough to penetrate among the beans, or we should probably have to record a successful discovery of the Spalding manuscript. In Harmony, the translation was pursued vigorously — and in three years the work was sent to the press. This time includes the ten months' suspension, on account of the abstraction of several sheets of the work by Mrs. Harris, who could not be induced by threat or cajolement to give them up. In order to evade this, the work is not what was first intended by the Lord : — and he received commandment to translate from an abridgment of the Plates of Nephi, instead of those of Lehi. It was revealed to him, that if he retranslated from the same plates, Satan would alter the first and publish them, and, being different, it would discredit the performance; but he was severely reprimanded for negligence in a revelation, and Cowdery sharply rebuked for impertinent curiosity, in wishing to see the golden plates, which was the prophets' privilege only.

But let us return to the consideration of the plan in view by this great work. There was a higher object than the making of money by it; — and another purpose, beyond harmonizing the Christian world.

The grand scheme was to convince the Jews in all the world that "Jesus is the Christ," their long-expected Messiah, as foretold by their ancient prophets. Accordingly, we find the prophecies here made perfectly plain. As Cyrus is spoken of in Isaiah by name long before his advent, so the name and office of the Savior is declared by the Nephite seers.

Nor was this all. The Indians throughout the length and breadth of the land were to be informed of their origin,— the cause of the divine wrath explained which had sunk them in degradation; — and that "in the last days" they could recover pristine favor, and again become a "fair and delightsome people," enjoying temporal salvation and eternal happiness. Could he succeed in making these two peoples believe in his book as a *divine record*, their conversion to Christianity was certain to follow. Nor was this thing beneath a soaring ambition, and its success would now place its author on the pinnacle of fame,— and the object to have been obtained was therefore a good one, whatever we may think of the deception attempted to be practised.

Even now do the Mormon missionaries apply to Jewish Rabbis, and ask them to listen to the voice of the gentile prophet, whose blood they aver has sealed the truth of his mission. We have lately seen the account of such a meeting at Amsterdam, but the Jew stands yet unconvinced and holds to his traditions; the Indian listens to "the talk" about the Great Spirit, and returns to the chase unconverted; — all these seem to view the matter as the fiction of an enthusiast.

The idea of founding a church with the new Seer as chief, does not, however, appear to have been entertained, until just before the printing the Book of Mormon. This was issued in 1830, and purports to give additional revelations of the dealings of God with his people, in the records that had been "hid up some fourteen hundred years before for preservation, but written for the Lamanites [Indians] a remnant of the house of Israel, and for Jew and Gentile, by the spirit of prophecy and revelation; to come forth, in due time, *by way of Gentile* * * * to the convincing of Jew and Gentile, that Jesus is the Christ, the Eternal God." This extract from the preface shows fully its character and purpose.

On the 6th of April of this year, the church, out of the Gentiles, was organized. There were but six members thus formed into the society, of which were, his father, and two brothers, and Cowdery, his scribe. From that time forth the Smith family rose from poverty to opulence. But nothing has fallen under our notice to show that the present hierarchy was then contemplated. Joseph was the first *Elder*, and Cowdery the second. In progress of time this expanded into two priesthoods; namely, the Melchisedek the Eternal one, which had two orders, the high priests and priests out of which was taken the Apostles and Council; — and the Aaronic, arranged into the various orders of elders, bishops, deacons, teachers, and so on. This is now the asserted imitation of the Primitive Apostolic Church, but if there is any resemblance of the office attached to the like names, we have seen no proof yet given.

It is related that Cowdery first baptised the prophet, and then the church had one commissioned to act; — and in the Book of Covenants the sponsors given are no less than the angels or spirits of Moses and Elias, and the Presidency of the first Christian church, Peter, James, and St. John in his own body, as he has never died. The "commissioned" prophet, now baptised and "commissioned" Elders, who began their enthusiastic preaching, and converted several visionary characters, persons without settled notions of theology, and likely to be carried away by the last fervid, popular harangue that should be addressed to them. Whole families were thus captivated, and the "New Revelation" and revival of the Old Church made much noise in the neighboring counties; and in a few months branches were organized in Fayette and Colesville, bodies which were mere associations however.

In the following August a Campbellite preacher, and one of some notoriety in Ohio, who was preaching notions and holding views of prophecy, restoration of the children of Israel and the Millennium, similar to those still taught in the Mormon society, made a visit to the State of New York and accidentally met with the Book of Mormon, and became convinced of its authenticity. This was the eloquent speaker, the pious song-poet, the enthusiastic Apostle, Parly P. Pratt. He is the author of many books of doctrine and history of persecutions among his people; and among those books is the "Voice of Warning to all Nations," which has done more in giving texts and establishing Mormonism than all the other publications of that people. This man is at present the chief of the "Stakes" in the Pacific islands. On his return to Ohio he presented the new bible to the still more enthusiastic and famed "Reformed Disciple," the ingenious and versatile Sidney Rigdon. He too adopted the new system; visited the Prophet and returned to call his society together, and then in a two hours' discourse of fervid eloquence, eloquent to those hearers, he expostulated, instructed, explained, and converted them; — he wept tears of sorrow and of joy over them, fell into swoons several times, and related visions of heaven to them. They became real fanatics.

It must be noted here that Rigdon had for three years already taught the literal interpretation of scripture prophecies, the gathering of the Israelites to receive the second coming, the literal reign of the Saints on earth, and the use of miraculous gifts in the church. From that visit of his to Joseph, do we date the Mormon organization of a church. In the conversations with Rigdon, the dawn of the morning gave place to the full light of the Sun, in the mind of its founder. Nothing yet had been written which forbade any method of discipline deemed expedient for the society; nor concerning doctrines which might not be interpreted to suit any circumstances. Accordingly we find "the Revelations" assuming a definite form. Rigdon is appointed expounder, and assigned an important post in the church; and soon is made the second person and great counsellor. But, in fact, he was the first in matters of theology, and wrote the Lectures on Faith, which preface the Book of Covenants and Doctrines, which were adopted by Smith, who purports to be the author, on the title-page. Since the apostasy of Rigdon, the faithful declare that he was once mighty in the faith, and a bright star in Zion, but, like Lucifer, has awfully fallen.

The conference of those two peculiar minds, spoken of above, was held in the autumn. In January following, a revelation is given, commanding those in the east to remove to the place which Rigdon had long since declared was on the borders of the "inheritance of the Saints, which extended thence to the Pacific." The prophet and his people removed to Kirtland, Ohio, where Pratt and Rigdon had already a society of over a thousand to receive them. New ardor and energy were infused, and such wonderful tales of visions, voices, and miracles were spread abroad, that people flocked from all parts of the lake region to witness and judge of this *new thing*. There were extacies—men and women falling to the floor in the public assemblies, wallowing, rolling, and tossing of hands — pointing into the heavens at the "cloud of witnesses" — uttering Indian dialects, and declaring that they would immediately convert them — there was swooning — rushing out of doors and running to the fields, some would mount stones and stumps, and speak in loud "tongues;" some would pick up the stones and read from characters of writing, which were miraculously made, and then suddenly disappeared — others found pieces of parchment falling upon them, which they declared were sealed with the seal of Christ, and which they no sooner copied than they vanished. The utmost excitement prevailed in their meetings, and it was all attributed to "the outpouring of the Spirit." The prophet himself seems to have become alarmed lest the "vision" should pass from him, and the vocation of Seer and Revelator become equally that of all. Accordingly he began to preach moderation, and finally informed them that it was the work of the devil, who was counterfeiting the gifts of the Spirit; and the faithful were cautioned to beware. Another revelation soon followed. This made the spiritual duties of the "Seer" so onerous, that he was told that strength to work would not be given him. He was to live "by the church," and through him alone was to come all the counsel of wisdom, and ghostly strength for the enlightenment of the same. He was privileged to converse with angels. All must obey him as the voice of the Most High, when the message was with the prefix "Thus saith the Lord," under the penalty of the Divine wrath.

CHAPTER II.

VARIOUS SETTLEMENTS, AND PROGRESS.

If the impulsiveness of the swooning Rigdon drove him occasionally to excess, in cooler moments he was the advocate of order and system. His was a restless character, between extremes. But the genius of Smith was a match for his ardor. In order to divert his attention and keep him in the traces, new and other work was carved out. A revelation is given in June, by which the principal elders, in parties of two, are directed west, to preach by the way and in the cities along their routes; and by a fixed time to meet on the borders of the Missouri. This mission was for selecting a site for a temple in the "land of Zion," and to found a city to be called Zion, the New Jerusalem of the Saints. This part of the country was chosen with great attention to its beauty of location, richness of soil, and all the requisites of a great empire. The point selected was near Independence, and where they were informed "from heaven," Adam's altar was built, and in the very centre of the Garden of Eden. Here it was supposed they could expand unmolested, and convert the sparse population over to their views, or buy out any unconvinced of the propriety of joining them. They sadly mistook the character of the pioneers of civilization, as the sequel proved.

The site for a city was selected, the land consecrated, and they proceeded to lay the corner-stone of the temple amid the beautiful groves which witnessed the Druidical pageantry. Here was to be the grand centre of gathering, and all other places of similar organization were to be called "Stakes of Zion"—here was the place where the kings of the earth were to bring their wealth, and the streets were to be paved with gold and precious stones. But as yet the "stakes" only flourish, while the consecrated "Zion" lies silent in the umbrageous forest groves on the banks of the great Missouri. "The everlasting residence" is yet uninhabited, and "the abodes of plenty and peace," the "joy of the whole earth," lie, as yet, in the peaceful silence of the wilderness.

The three hundred missionaries forwarded their converts hither, and there was soon collected over 1200 in Jackson County and the vicinity, buying lands and cultivating them peaceably. The heads of the church returned, shortly after the ceremony of laying the corner-stone, to Shinehar, as they now named the Kirtland "stake," and engaged in building a temple there, laying off a city, and offering town lots for sale. All property was consecrated to the Lord, and the doctrine laid down, that the Saints were only stewards of what they had in charge, and that a tenth part of all, labor; earnings, and time, should be dedicated forthwith, and for ever, to the use of the priesthood, under direction of the Presidency. Public store-houses were erected to receive the tithes and donations, and the bishops put in charge of the collection.

Two years thus passed quietly away in the temporal matters, though strifes and apostacies became alarmingly frequent in spiritual concerns. Opportunely for the waning power of the prophet, a turmoil appeared in Zion, and persecution came to his aid, and cemented the union among those not anathematised. The people in Jackson County collected and drove out the Mormons, their neighbors, who were obliged to take refuge across the river: but they refused to sell their lands, which belonged to the "Saints of the Lord," and they could not alienate them. When Joseph heard of these troubles, he sent forth a revelation, which informed his people that Heaven was visiting for their lack of faith, strifes and disagreements, but that he would chastise and return them again to their inheritance. To make this good, a party called the "Army of Zion" left Ohio to aid their brethren, being armed and drilled for the service; but before they arrived on the ground, the mob, or a party of militia, met them and demanded a parley. As the heavens opened not in vengeance on the enemy, the prophet disbanded his party instead of fighting, and his demonstration not having the effect of awing the country into submission, the holy soldiery dispersed. Some of these remained in Missouri, joining their brethren; others returned to Ohio, but many fell with the cholera. This last was declared to be the fulfilling of prophecy, for "judgment must begin at the house of God," but it was to pass thence and utterly destroy their enemies.

The attack upon those in Jackson County appears to have been without provocation, other than fears of their clanship. There had been no complaint of misdemeanors, and this expulsion, without color of law, was most unjust and oppressive. The following year, 1834, a guard was furnished by the Governor, and an attempt to secure redress was made in the courts, but the mobocratic spirit was so prevalent that the attorney-general advised the abandonment of the suit, and the civil proceedings were given up accordingly.

More peaceable times now seemed to hover over the Mormon fortunes. They gathered rapidly together in Clay and adjoining counties, and pressed forward their farming operations vigorously; and plenty again appeared on their tables, and comfort in their dwellings. At Kirtland, in the autumn of 1835, a Hebrew and theological school was formed, and several hundred elders attended the instructions given by a celebrated Hebraist and scholar. In the following spring, several of these now learned doctors repaired to Missouri, and large accessions flocked in from abroad, which so alarmed the old inhabitants of Clay County, that they determined to drive them away. The evident clanship and unity of action in all matters, caused these new comers to be distrusted. Various conferences were held, and consulting committees appointed, during the year, and finally an arrangement was made, by which it was stipulated that the Mormons should withdraw to Caldwell, if lands were procured in exchange for those they should leave; and the affair was amicably arranged, and the removal effected. Here, in the hope of a permanent residence, they set to work again with more than usual ardor.

Meanwhile swimming operations in lots, buildings, banks, and manufactures, were in full tide at Kirtland. A large mercantile house was started on a tithe basis, and obtained credit to a considerable amount; and in 1837 a bank was set in motion, and property assumed fictitious values. The temple, with its various compartments for giving and receiving endowments, or for imparting and obtaining the gifts of the Spirit, was so far advanced that the rites were actually held. For some days wine flowed freely — wine that had been consecrated, and declared by the prophet to be harmless and not intoxicating. This, with previous fastings, and expectations wrought up to the highest pitch, and other means used to create mental excitement, produced unheard of effects, if we may credit the witnesses of these proceedings. Visions, tongues, trances, wallowings on the ground, shoutings, weeping, and laughing, the outpouring of prophecies, and terrible cursings of the Missourians, exhortations from house to house, and preaching to unseen nations; these, and other fantastic things, were among "the signs following" at Kirtland.

Not long after followed the crash of the speculations. The improvident habits of sudden wealth, the unwise investments in lots, houses, and mills, and the loose management of the mercantile firm, brought on embarrassments in 1838. The bank failed, and the managers were prosecuted for swindling. Smith and Rigdon secretly departed for far-west, the new Zion, and thus escaped to "the city of refuge," from the sheriff and his writs, and perhaps from the penitentiary. Here they imparted to the Saints the *developing* nature of their own spirits. New cities were located, and settlements begun in Davies, Caldwell, and Carroll counties. The spot where Adam blessed his children was revealed, and a city was founded in the valley, to be called Adam-mon-diamon, significant of the patriarchal blessing.

CHAPTER III.

CONTENTIONS IN MISSOURI.

THE leaders began to feel confident of sustaining any desirable measures and ruling the counties. Their followers had greatly increased, and were obedient to their will. They now injudiciously boasted of their power, and proclaimed that hereafter they should not submit to vexatious lawsuits, nor yield to the violence of mobs. The favor of the Almighty was on their side, and "one could chase a thousand." On the other hand, the older inhabitants complained of the loss of property, and alleged that no confidence could be placed in contracts made with the Mormons. When credit was given, they could not find the persons to collect dues: fictitious names were used to obtain goods and chattels, and when enquiries were made for certain persons, nobody could be found who ever heard of them. Also they began to fear that the doctrine of the Saints' right to property, would render their possessions insecure. Crimination and recrimination became frequent and mutual. But we may readily believe that the fears of the Missourians were more aroused on the prospect of losing political ascendency. In their meetings to consult on the alarming state of affairs, they resolved that "the rule of the counties should never be submitted to the control of Joseph Smith."

Peace and prosperity had given leisure for more sober reflection to the thoughtful and sincere among the Mormons. They began to consider the tendency of their doctrines, the uncharitableness of their principles, and the consequences to result from exclusive clanship; but more than this, the truthfulness of the leaders and claims of their prophet. The result was, that many dissented and joined in the sentiments of their neighbors. These were hated and feared far more than those styled Gentiles; and to expel the "traitors," as well as to guarantee and protect against open enemies, the chief persons organized a secret society, with signs and "Key-words," called the Big Fan, and afterwards known as the Danites. These were sworn to obey the Presidency in all things, right or wrong; and drive off, or put out of sight in a mysterious manner, all who were obnoxious or irretrievably lost, to them; and suspicious strangers in Far West were to be removed. That persons suddenly disappeared or "slipped their breath" is often affirmed by them selves, but they say they were horse-thieves and vile wretches, who left society for its good.

The sanguine preaching of enthusiastic priests had infused boasting valor into the mass, and a warlike tone pervaded all classes against any who should attack them or dispute their pretensions,—the same as now prevails in the mountains against the ideas of oppression. Rigdon became excessively violent, and taught the Saints that they must expect to fight;—that traitors must be dealt with according to the law of the Lord, instancing the fate of Judas, whose bowels, he said, were trampled out by the Apostles; and Ananias and Sapphira, who were killed by Peter. In a fourth of July oration, commended by the prophet in his Journal published among them, he threw down the gauntlet to the State and all opposers, and pronounced, "woe to them, in the name of Jesus Christ." They declared themselves able to march through the Capital, and if the mob obliged them to fight, they would not stop until St. Louis was in their possession. It would seem that the disgrace of failing to build Zion, as predicted, and the insults and injuries already received, had wrought up this leader, and those kindred in spirit, to desperation; and perceiving the mobocratic feeling rising a third time, they desired to overawe it, if possible, by a threatening demonstration, or stake their fortunes on the hazards of a war to the knife, by which they might clear the neighborhood of the disaffected; and on the plea of self-defence, afterward make peaceable terms with the State authorities When such dispositions existed on both sides, causes "light as air" could bring them into collision; and mutual acts of plunder and retaliation became frequent. At an election of county officers an open fracas began. The Mormons drove off their opponents, and confiscated property, and burnt some houses, after driving women and children into the woods, where considerable suffering prevailed; — in one or two instances children were born of houseless and terror-stricken mothers. A company of militia was called together and were encamped on a small river, and were there attacked by a party of Mormons, and some killed; they supposing the troops to be a mob marching to destroy their property.

Complaints of these seditions were made to Governor Boggs, and he ordered out the State troops to enforce order upon all the citizens; — even, if it was found necessary, to exterminate the obnoxious Mormons, who were presumed to be the fomenters of the discord. The principal leaders were secured, and a trial was had before Judge King; and Smith, Rigdon, and P. P. Pratt incarcerated. For the evidence and proceedings of this trial, the testimony of citizens, dissenters, and Mormons, reference must be made to the official publication of the State and that of the United States Senate. We are here dealing with events, and leave every person curious to know the truth or falsity of the causes of this war, to form his own opinion.

But in the account given by the Apostle Pratt (which is not there to be found) we have a picture of horrors and inhumanity toward his people which would surpass our belief, if we did not know that a lawless mob were the actors in the scenes, or an uncontrolled, exasperated soldiery. There were too many authenticated facts that make the blood curdle as we contemplate them, to deny that foul injustice was often practised; — and the deeds of savage brutality, whose disgusting details we pass in silence, make us sigh that they could be enacted by American citizens. Pratt avers that the flesh of their martyred comrades was cooked and offered to the prisoners in jail for food. At How's mills, twenty of his brethren were lulled into fancied security by professions of friendship, and when defenceless in a log building at night, they were coolly shot, through the crevices; — and after the massacre, they found a lad of nine years of age, concealed under a forge, and, dragging him out, deliberately blew off the top of his head,

— the miscreant boasting of his manly prowess, and all dancing with the exultation of fiends incarnate.

The prisoners were carried from one jail to another, and their trial for treason delayed; their sufferings greatly enhanced from the uncertainty which hung over the fate of their wives and children. At last these leaders escaped; while on one of the journeys, the guard sank into a deep sleep after a drunken frolic, and thence they found their way to Illinois, to join those who had preceded them.

The Mormons had been driven from the state. The sufferings of that defenceless multitude, whose arms and property had been surrendered, as they crossed the State to Commerce, on the Mississippi, over the bleak prairies, and amid the storms of wind and snow, in November, were most intense. The aged and the young, the sick and the delicate women, the infants, and even those born on the road, houseless and unsheltered, were to be seen in that crowd of forlorn, persecuted, and unresisting exiles. The rivers were without bridges, the waters flowed with chilling anchor ice, the currents, swollen by recent rains, had to be forded or swum, as the delay of bridging would kill by starvation or cold. Thirty or more persons had been murdered, others were sinking under exposure, grief, and hardship; and as one was relieved by death, a bark coffin would enclose him, and a wave of the prairie sea pass over the mortal remains, and the sad cortege move on. Families were scattered, widows with helpless children clinging to them, and piteously clamoring for food; hunger, want, and disease through all ranks—this was the exodus of a people under an inclement sky, from their homes of plenty and comfort. That fearful journey was made where fuel could scarcely be found to cook the scanty stores, and where cattle died of starvation, for they could not be trusted to range far for grass, and must be tethered at night, nor permitted leisure to graze by day, but convey along the starving pilgrims to a place of refuge. All that brotherly kindness can do, was exhibited then — the crust was shared with the first neighbor whose store was exhausted, the robust cheered the weak, and the hearts of all united in sympathy

But what have not those persecutors to answer for? There is One who hath said, "vengeance is mine, I will repay," and if he that steals must restore fourfold, surely he that causes a pang of human suffering, cannot expect less than a like retribution in the future of Providence.

Twelve thousand persons arrived on the banks of the Mississippi in destitute plight; their tale of distress touched the hearts of the Illinoisians, and they hospitably received them. Provisions and clothing were hastily gathered and freely bestowed—this generous conduct is a bright ray, piercing through the murky clouds of that dark tragedy.

Let us reflect a moment on what has been presented before us. Can we blame a sad, revengeful remembrance of those times by the Mormons? We may ask them to forgive—to forget, never. And has a remuneration been made them for the wholesale spoliations of those whose crime was laid in their mistaken view of the rights of conscience? We have heard of none. But we have heard that one appeared in Jackson County to sue out a writ of possession of his land, and the citizens collected and stamped him under their feet, until his bowels gushed out, and then buried him; this was all the homestead he secured. Such exhibitions of justice do not satisfy the mountain brethren that purity and right prevail in Missouri—yet, afar off, they are preparing memorials, praying permission to return, and fondly hope yet to possess the heart-beloved Zion.

Those who misled the credulous multitude in the war should have been punished. After the first conflict, they declared the war must derive its support from their opponents, and consecrated their cattle, hogs, and honey to their own use, under the names of "buffalo, and bear-meat, and olive oil." These contributions from the Gentiles were gathered by an armed band called the Fur Company, as indemnifications for losses sustained by the mobs. They forcibly drove out people, and inflicted some of the misery which they afterwards endured in their own exodus. We may admit that the rulers were corrupt, and ambitious of ruling that part of the country—these could have been secured and punished, and the innocent, deluded ones, saved from the awful misery which awaited them. To those surviving those times, a semblance of compensation can be made by giving them the cultivated lands of their mountain homes — it could only be a show of gift, for there they have well earned their comforts in toil and battle against Indian marauders.

This expulsion of the Mormons from one State to another in the closing months of 1838, is here stated as an historical fact; and it may show that this century is not so much advanced in philanthropy, that it will tolerate error of opinion without question, or that it seeks to correct it only by argument, and the enlightenment of general education. There is great need of progress in charity, and the knowledge of treating what is ridiculous by letting it fall into contempt without notice. Crime may be punished and restrained by what raises folly into wisdom in the estimation of thousands.

This violence in Missouri gave a new impetus to Mormonism. The people were concentrated thereby, and unanimity of views and opinions again prevailed. The dissenters were driven away — the weak in faith were made strong, under the harangues of teachers who loudly proclaimed that so "Christ and his Apostles were made to suffer." They were to pass through like tribulation. But something more confirmed them. They had assumed the name and were included under the ban of extermination. After the storm arose, it was too late to evade the consequences; — they could not recant and receive favor with the mob. No credit would be, or was given to defections made under such circumstances,— it was looked upon as a ruse in order to save their property, and they were not trusted. Root and branch must be cleared away.

Thus, every thing conspired to make them twofold more the children of Mormonism than before. And this, we observe, has been the case with several dissenters. They have gone back to the first love: — they feel a stigma rests on them for having once joined that belief, and their vanity is more powerful than their judgment. These "brands from the burning" are received with open arms, for they show that other religions are unsatisfactory, and they are the proud trophies of victory of the new religion;— no wonder that the unstable seek for peace, in a delusion that treats them so kindly. Even the most notorious, such as Rigdon and Cowdery, former members of the first dynasty, have been invited to return, we are informed.

It is remarkable that the wife of the Prophet, "Emma, the Elect Lady," according to his Revelation, and the first three witnesses to the Book of Mormon, who affirm that "an angel came down from heaven" and laid the golden plates "before their eyes" and that "the voice of God" declared the truth of them in their hearing; also the chief of the Eight witnesses who declare with "words of truth and soberness" they handled them with their hands; together with Martin Harris and the Editor of the Gospel Messenger, and some of the ablest advocates of the doctrines in earlier times,— have left the society, without apparently affecting the faith or enthusiasm of the later converts. It was when these men were leaving that the Danite band was formed to *fan* them, and keep their mouths closed, and others from deserting,— they were the fruits of peace and prosperity.

CHAPTER IV.

SETTLEMENT AT NAUVOO.

WHEN the homeless starving multitudes had crossed the Mississippi, and found solace in Illinois, the question of a new residence arose, and the site of the town of Commerce, in the elbow-bend of the river, was selected for a city, and lands purchased on the half-breed tract, in Iowa, opposite. The name given to the place was Nauvoo, The City of Beauty. The situation was offered to the Prophet by Dr. Galland, the owner, who is the reputed author of a letter to Smith, setting forth the peculiar advantages of this point as a nucleus for his increasing colony. The plan for a city and temple is most ably set forth as a capital for a religious empire; and that a commercial town would be well supported by the surrounding country, which is rich in agricultural resources. It is situated at the head of the Des Moines rapids, and beautiful prairies extend, like the undulating ocean, as far as the eye can reach, from the highest ridges, on all sides. On the rich delta of the Des Moines and Father of Waters, and in Hancock county, another "everlasting residence" for the saints, was consecrated. Soon the colonists changed the desert to an abode of plenty and richness. Gardens sprang up, as by magic, decorated with the most beautiful flowers of the old and new world, whose seeds were brought as mementoes from former homes, by the converts that flocked to the new stake of Zion. Broad streets were soon fenced, houses erected, and the busy hum of industry heard in the marts of commerce: — the steamboat unladed its stores and passengers, and departed for a fresh supply of merchandize,— fields waved with the golden harvests, and cattle dotted the rolling hills. A temple site was chosen on the brow of the bluff overlooking the lower town, which part of the city was on the sloping meadow in the bend below. The pattern was given to the prophet by his angel, and all the details explained orally. A gentile architect was employed to draft it by dictation. He soon found that it was complicated and broke the rules of his art; but notwithstanding his difficulties, Joseph insisted that the *tout ensemble* must be right; and, true enough, the "Lord's design" was at last pronounced correct. Revelations were freely vouchsafed, and they were informed that their situation was much better than what it was in Pandemonium; and they must bear the late chastisement like obedient children. All saints were loudly called to pay in their tithes of time and money — and one revelation, especially, told the kings and queens to become nursing parents to the church, and bring in their gold, their silver, and all precious stones, to build and adorn the temple. Minute transactions were governed by these revelations; — some of them have been printed, but many more remain in the manuscript, and are of no further use than historical records for preserving memorials of that time, and actions of that people.

Flourishing centres of dense settlements sprung up in the vicinity of Nauvoo, and the accessions and exertions of emigrants enlarged their borders. Not alone to these was the increase confined. Horse-thieves and house-breakers,— robbers and villains gathered there to cloak their deeds in mystery, who, caring nothing for religion, could take the appearance of baptism, and be among, but not of them. Speculators came in, and bought lots, with the hope of great remuneration, as the colony increased. The latter class, unwilling to pay tithes, soon fell into disrepute, and when proper time had elapsed for conversion without effect, measures were taken to oust them. A proper sum would be offered for their improvements and land, and if not accepted, then petty annoyances were resorted to. One of these was called "whittling off." Three men would be deputed and paid for their time to take their jack-knives and sticks,— down-east Yankees of course,—and sitting down before the obnoxious man's door, begin their whittling. When the man came out they would stare at him, but say nothing. If he went to the market, they followed and whittled. Whatever taunts, curses, or other provoking epithets were applied to them, no notice would be taken, no word spoken in return, no laugh on their faces. The jeers and shouts of street urchins made the welkin ring, but deep silence pervaded the whittlers. Their leerish look followed him every where, from "morning dawn to dusky eve." When he was in-doors, they sat patiently down, and assiduously performed their jack-knife duty. Three days are said to have been the utmost that human nature could endure of this silent annoyance; the man came to terms, sold his possessions for what he could get, or emigrated to parts unknown.

Though the banks of the river at Nauvoo are dry, and the city site rises in an abrupt slope to a commanding eminence on the prairie level, the marshes below exhaled a miasm that brought on its breath the "ague fiend," and much distressed those who had been exposed on the wintry march, and the new comers, whilst acclimating. During the process of draining the marshes, and in four years, one third of their number perished. This is another charge laid to their persecutors by the later converts, who say they forced them to take up their residence where no one was expected to be able to live, and allowed them to remain, only to see them perish. But numbers survived the agues, and the place was assuming a healthy, pleasant aspect. The State favored the exiles; charters were obtained for the city, with peculiarly favorable privileges — the Nauvoo Legion was incorporated, and the arms of the State loaned, in which they were well drilled, and became a standing army, with the prophet as Lieutenant General —the chiefs were incorporated a company for building the temple, and other companies for a grand boarding-house, the result of a revelation, in which the prophet and family were provided with an elegant suite of apartments, free of expense "*for ever*"—for a university, and for manufactures.

General conferences were semi-annually held for awhile, and missionaries appointed to Palestine, Africa, and Europe, and to each congressional district of the home country. The policy was, and always has been, to select the ambitious, the uneasy, or the too enquiring and knowing ones, and, under Divine command, send them to carry the revived gospel to the ends of the earth, in order to give them a chance to let off the steam of discontent. Especially it is the policy to put on this duty inquisitive minds who are diving too deeply into the mysteries of their faith, and are "becoming weak in the same." Such usually receive the command "from on high," to buckle on the armor, as a particular compliment of Heaven — and, flattered by the notice of the great President above, accept the commission, and go forth to battle manfully. They become oftentimes the most zealous advocates, for, being thrown on the defensive, they seek for arguments to sustain what just before they were disposed to overthrow; and disputation and controversy confirm them wonderfully in the truth of the doctrine, and their power to "confound the wise and the unwise." It is the surest way to make full Mormons of the wavering, by enlisting their pride, and engaging their attention on the defensive side of the question. They soon look into their own souls for the proof that they are on the side of truth, as their convictions go with their desire of proselyting. "We know it, for the evidence is revealed within us," they will say — the *interior proof* is all in all, when the historical or theological opposition is found too strong to be met with argument.

Missionaries are sent with all the promptness of military orders, a three days' notice for a three years' absence from family and business not unfrequently being all that is given. Families are cared for by the Presidency and bishops. Three hundred were chosen at one conference. Previous to starting, they were assembled to receive the orders of Joseph. He preached a fervid sermon, that stimulated their pride of conquering difficulties without scrip or purse. One of that band, still well-affected to the society, though differing on one point from its teaching, related to the writer some parts of the discourse. One main point insisted on was, that "spiritual wifery" was to be most pointedly denied; and that they taught that one man should live in chaste fidelity with one woman in conjugal relationship. In the dark concerning the revelation allowing polygamy, he sincerely declared that but one wife was ever known to any of his brethren. While zealously preaching in the city of New York, he was thought worthy, by the Apostle Lyman, to be let into the secret of the "blessings of Jacob," the privileges of the Saints. Called aside one day by the President of the Stake, he was told that God had always rewarded his distinguished saints with special privileges, such as would be wrong for sinners, but by revelation made harmless to the good. As an instance he would cite Jacob, David, and Solomon, who had many wives allowed them. In these last days, also, the like had been accorded to Joseph Smith and others; and having now full confidence in his holiness, the priest could have the same privilege of adding to the household of the faith many children, by choosing additions to the present wife. The priest says he was utterly astounded, but, on reflection, chose to dissemble, and say he would consider the matter. In the evening he was invited to witness "a sealing" of several couples, at a large boarding-house. In the front parlor the ceremony, like a marriage, was performed; and, as each pair was "finished" by the priest, they retired through the folding doors, and thus to their own apartments. The guest was so shocked, that he retired to his home, and though he never took any open part against the "church of new privileges," he was denounced as a deserter in their papers, and the public cautioned against him as a defamer. Strange to say, he was, at the time of our interview, contemplating rejoining his people in the mountains.

POLYGAMY.

It was during this peaceful time, about 1841–2, that the *revelation* allowing to the High Priests and chiefs of their hierarchy as many wives as they could support, and declaring it a duty for those eligible to the priesthood, to take one wife at least, was said to be given. In vain, it is reported, proved the opposition of Emma, The Elect Lady — in vain, also, her threat of another husband in retaliation; the only consolation received was, that a prophet must obey the Lord, "he would be obedient to the heavenly vision." The story of "spiritual wives," or rather that the wives were held in common, and those whose husbands were not in full fellowship with the church, like themselves, were sealed to the elders, probably arose from the published doctrine that a woman cannot be saved without a man to take her into the heavenly kingdom. It is even yet asserted, we believe, by the *Mormonish*, and opposers of this part of "Relevation," (for there are many of both sexes denouncing it, without being cut off, because it is not yet a publicly proclaimed doctrine,) that certain women are sealed to high dignitaries; but, for ourselves, we know nothing of the truth or falsity of the charge: we can only say that all marriage relations that came under our notice were most purely correct in appearance; and that all wives in Utah showed a devotion and alacrity in domestic affairs and family duties, that would promote the harmony of the world, and make many a heavy heart beat for joy, if universal.

That polygamy existed at Nauvoo, and is now a matter scarcely attempted to be concealed among the Mormons, is certain. Elsewhere are given their reasons for its justification. It is a thing of usual and general conversation in the mountains, and we often heard one of the Presidency spoken of with his twenty-eight wives; another with "forty-two, more or less;" and the third called an old bachelor, because he has only a baker's dozen. It is neither reproach nor scandal; no one is present to see the ceremony of sealing but the priestly clerk and parties; therefore, if a Gentile asks one if all the women in his neighbor's house, with prattling babes, are the landlord's wives, the answer is, "I know nothing about it, and attend to no man's family relations."

CHAPTER V.

POLITICAL MOVEMENTS—MURDER OF JOSEPH.

THE Mormons now boasted of having a hundred thousand persons in the faith throughout the States; and this accounts for the silence of the press concerning them, as their vote was a balancing power. They would go in a body on political questions. Smith visited Washington, and reports his interview with the President to have concluded with this emphatic assertion of Mr. Van Buren; "Sir, your cause is just, but I can do nothing for you." In view of the approaching election of '44, letters were written to the prominent candidates, and answers elicited, which Joseph pronounced unsatisfactory, for no one pledged to coerce Missouri to restore Zion and their lands to them, as Latter-Day Saints. Then the prophet sent forth his "Views on Government," advocated a National Bank, denounced all punishment for desertions in the army or navy, throwing the soldier on his honor alone; would pardon out every convict from the penitentiaries; curtail government offices and pay; reduce the number of representatives; and, in short, make every thing harmonious and prosperous, by declaring that all were free to try "honesty" and "love" in their dealings, and become a brotherhood. Joseph was put in nomination for the Presidency; and the Mormons assert, that had he lived for the next trial after, he would have been elected. The opportunity was not given. A dark day was approaching. Their neighbors became dissatisfied and jealous. Their property disappeared, and causes tried in the Nauvoo courts went always against them. No Mormon could be brought to justice, they said. Political aspirations were alleged also; that they aspired to rule the State, and, under a spiritual leader, set the laws at defiance. It was industriously circulated that thieves, "bogus makers," and robbers, were harbored, protected, and assisted by the leaders. Cattle and utensils disappeared from the neighboring farms. Traces of stolen property were obtained at Nauvoo.

But, more than all, intestine quarrels brought on the crisis of affairs. Many influential and talented persons, finding themselves deceived both in the sanctity of the prophet, and in advancing their temporal fortunes, deserted his standard, and denounced him for licentiousness, drunkenness, and tyranny. Women impeached him of attempted seduction; which his apology that it was merely to see if they were virtuous, could not satisfy. Criminations brought back recriminations against certain men. The Wasp, Joseph's paper, lashed the dissenters with bitter hatred. The dissenters established a counter battery in the Expositor, and published one number, detailing the most offensive debaucheries on the part of the prophet and his principal friends.

The city council was convened, and eleven members of the twelve voted the Expositor a nuisance. A party immediately destroyed the press, scattering the type in the streets, and burning all of the edition it could find. Those engaged in the work repaired to head-quarters, and were complimented by Joseph and Hyrum for doing their duty to the Lord, being further assured that they should be rewarded.

Writs were issued against the mob leaders and abettors, but they were immediately set at liberty by Habeas Corpus, a process often resorted to, whereby the outsiders could never bring such to justice. The officer then procured a writ in the county, and summoned a posse to enforce the law—but the people and troops in Nauvoo prevented it, and when the militia were called out, Joseph, as mayor and commanding general of the Nauvoo Legion, declared the city under martial law. The Governor of the State was appealed to, who repaired to Carthage, the county seat, and ordered out three companies of the State militia, and for a time a collision seemed inevitable. The Governor sent an agent to the Smiths, assuring their personal safety, and called upon them to meet him in conference. Joseph sent two men, Bernhisel and Taylor, to confer with Governor Ford—but the latter despatched an officer with the militia to arrest the prophet and patriarch. These crossed over the Mississippi into Iowa, to watch events, keeping up by boat a correspondence with the council. Finding that their own people were being incensed at their desertion, by advice of council it was concluded best to obey the summons of the Governor, their friends feeling sure of acquittal on trial. Accordingly they came back and started for Carthage, but, on the way, met a party with an order to disband the Legion, and deliver up the State arms. They returned with the troops, and the order was duly executed.

They now repaired to Carthage, and were indicted for treason, and lodged in jail, with two others, Dr. Richards and John Taylor, of the Apostles. The dissenters and those who had suffered loss of property were greatly exasperated against them; and those whose families were dishonored, or attempts upon them made, swore dire vengeance. But the Governor, seeing things apparently quiet, and the leaders safely secured, discharged the troops, and went to Nauvoo and addressed the people, advising submission to the course of the laws, and to demean themselves as good citizens, and justice should be done to all parties.

On the 27th of June, 1844, he started back, and on the way met an express, informing him that a horrible massacre of the Smiths had been committed by the mob, in whom the spirit of revenge had been roused, and satiated in blood. The Governor, fearing that the Mormons would at once destroy the inhabitants, advised them to evacuate the place, and putting General Deming in command of the few troops that could be raised, retired forthwith to Quincy, to await the sequel of events.

It appears that when the troops were disbanded, many individuals conspired with other citizens to attack the jail and take justice into their own hands. Early in the day they assaulted the door of the room in which the prisoners were incarcerated. Richards and Taylor, lying on the floor, made a stretch across the room, the feet of one against the shoulders of the other, and kept the door from fully opening. Guns were thrust in and discharged, and Joseph, with a revolver, returned two shots, hitting one man in the elbow. A ball struck Hyrum the patriarch, and he fell ex claiming, "I am killed!"—to which Joseph replied, "O brother Hyrum!" The prophet then threw up the window, and, in the act of leaping through was killed by balls fired from the outside, saying as he fell, "O Lord, my God." The people in the hall forced into the room and wounded Taylor; the other escaped "without a hole in his robe."

Thus ended the mortal career of one whose true biography has yet to be written. He founded a dynasty which his death rendered more secure, and sent forth principles that take fast hold on thousands in all lands; and the name of Great Martyr of the Ninteenth century, is a tower of strength to his followers. He lived fourteen years and three months after founding a society with six members, and could boast of having one hundred and fifty thousand ready to do his bidding when he died; all of whom regarded his word as the voice from Heaven. Among his disciples he bears a character for talent, uprightness, and purity, far surpassing all other men with whom they ever were acquainted, or whose biography they have read. But few of these admirers were cognizant of other than his prophetic career, and treat with scornful disdain all that is said in disparagement of his earlier life. With those who knew him in his youth, and have given us solemn testimony, he is declared an indolent vagabond, an infamous liar of consummate impudence. He is regarded by the "Gentiles" who saw him in the last few years of successful power, to have been a man of unbridled lust, and engaged with the counterfeiting and robbing bands of the Great Valley, but these charges have never been substantiated—and dissenters charge him with breaking the whole decalogue.

His mind was an active one, and he possessed elements of an engaging kind; without them he could not have held men so long and so forcibly. In this, he has compeers among those who have played a similar part on the credulity of mankind, and claimed divine mission. Like them, he was bold in assertion of his "truths" and hurled anathemas upon all who did not acknowledge his pretensions. He found many to listen, who would then consider and examine awhile, and ask themselves the question, "what, after all, if this should be true?"—and in that *doubt* lay their danger, for "he that doubteth is damned" when the true light is shining around him. The wonder that strikes us is, the time and the manner in which this new doctrine is sought to be established, and its rapid success. No one can doubt that there was genius, sagacity, and intuitive insight into the characters of men, which was operated with from the time of inducing Harris to assist in publishing his bible. From the moment that person was duped, and became bound by his cupidity to the issue of the book from the press, was the struggle of mental power. Next, when it was found that the work would not be a lucrative object, what but transcendent ability could have controlled the mind of the versatile, eloquent, and methodical Rigdon, and used his talents to organize a church system and put it into complete operation, which no follower has dared to amend? And the most bitter trials did not daunt him; he looked calmly on the misery of thousands about him, in the fires of persecution, and still moved on, unflinching, till at last he dared a ruthless mob to his death, which showed a determination to ride "the whirlwind and direct the storm," regardless of the human suffering that might be endured.

The anecdotes of his eccentricities and manners are household themes in the mountains, and time and distance are embellishing them with all the virtues of the true hero. They love to relate to listening friends and children how the prophet Joseph would strip off the mask of hypocrisy—how he would meet a new convert, bringing his long-faced piety from the other denominations, and challenge a wrestling match in the streets, nor let off the sanctimonious and surprised fellow until he had shown him that his athletic reputation was not a sham, by leaving him flat in the dust—and to all he taught that his was a laughter-loving, cheerful religion. And how another, coming with charitable zeal to the prophet, would be requested to lend for the temple all his money, and then be noticed no more than other strangers; the poor destitute being obliged to shoulder spade and axe, and labor in poverty, until he would decamp or be proved faithful. If he stood the test for a few months, he would suddenly be called to head-quarters, and eligible lots assigned him, and some position given in which he could earn his bread in comfort.

That he had become politically as well as religiously ambitious, is apparent from his letters on governmental policy. By establishing "stakes" in various places, he could hope to hold the balance of power between the two great parties, and ultimately force one to help his own people to place him in the highest office in the nation. It is evident, that had he been permitted to colonize in Missouri, in a few years the control of the State must have passed into his hands. After the expulsion, all his movements and sentiments were tending toward regaining that lost section, and his credit with the people depended on fulfilling the prophecy concerning Zion. It is a cardinal point in the preaching of his successor, and in view of having to fight for it, that there is still kept up the drilling of *the Legion*, and exercises in military tactics, until there is in that community the material for the best partisan troops in the world. The mantle of the modern assumed Elijah has fallen on his kindred Elisha, whose ambition, though not as wide, has the same determined purpose of dominion as that of Joseph the Seer.

His death by violence, and by his enemies, was opportune for the support of the system he sought to establish. He had arrived at that point in the revolution which he led, when the least delay would have caused its waves to flow over and engulf him. New things and new light were constantly expected by those whose credulity was the measure of their faith — they were taught to look for principles according as they admitted and acted by them. Hence the immense strides in the last year toward pantheism and materialism of the Deities. And aspiring men were also bringing forward revelations which they were not content should be attributed to the inspiration of Beelzebub. Rigdon had again established his chain of communication with the angels of the unseen world — Bishop had accumulated large folios of enlightened "table-talk" with the spirits unseen, and Strang had found him self commissioned a King of Saints, and felt the divine inflatus within; and the numerous contradictions in the revelations of the prophet, though explained on the principle *that God gave according to altered circumstances,* threw doubt on the prophet's own. The endeavor to apply this to the relation of the sexes, and make that innocent which all the enlightened world considered wrong, by merely his assertion that "thus saith the Lord," staggered the faith of the virtuous who were not too blinded to reflect or think for themselves. This it was that commenced the quarrel which ended in his arrest and death.

He lived long enough for his fame, and died when he could just be called a martyr. He had become too violent and impatient, to control, for a long time, the multitude — he could begin, but not conduct, successfully, a revolution. In this respect, he contrasts remarkably with his successor in the Seership of the Saints. The latter could never be a martyr. His prudence and foresight have been shown under the most trying circumstances, and in cool calculation of the future he is pre-eminent, and plans with cautious policy to meet all the exigencies before him. Policy is a word little known in the vocabulary of the first prophet, and is the most frequent in that of the present one. It galls the more simple-hearted ones however, and they sigh for the bold attitude of the first Presidency, and feel derelict to the duties of their divine mission by yielding at all to the political interference of the general government — waiting impatiently for the signal to march back to Zion — yet, on their principles of obeying "counsel," restraining themselves to yield a temporary submission.

BRIGHAM YOUNG ELECTED.

The murder of their prophet exasperated the people of Nauvoo. They were ready, and a vast majority determined, on immediate war to the knife, with all engaged in that horrid tragedy, or whoever might come to abet them. A few more sagacious minds perceived the danger of such a course, and began skilfully to prevent the utter ruin of their hopes, likely to result from open hostility to the state. They harangued them on the stand, and talked with the clubs collected at the corners of the streets. The great drum was beating to arms. It was a fearful struggle, that going on in the breasts of the prudent. Revenge was deep in every heart, and the bursting movement there was interpreted into the voice of the Holy Spirit; and it was made audible in the terrible curses poured forth on the Gentile murderers. The "time to fight," was, by most, supposed to have come. But skilful delays were interposed by the influential: their arms had been just surrendered and a new organization made, and leaders were to be chosen. The day passed off and no companies had started, and wrath was bosomed for the morrow. In the morning after, the congregation was early collected at the temple-square or gathering place. The chief Apostles promised them the vengeance of heaven upon their enemies, but that they were not quite ripe enough for the vials of wrath to empty their torments upon them. Shortly the pestilence, the fire, and the sword, would do their work.

The funeral pageant next absorbed all their attention. The mourning was sore, sad, and deep over the beloved patriarch Hyrum and the adored prophet Joseph. In "their deaths they were not divided,'' and, among the songs of Zion heard in the Mormon worshipping assemblies, are the elegy and the poeans of Joseph and Hyrum, the martyrs for their faith, but triumphant in glory.

The struggle for the leadership, the Seer succession, followed. Rigdon, as second in rank claimed promotion; also by former revelations declared himself assigned to be their prophet. He called a meeting and proclaimed his position as head. He gave a revelation, by which he was commanded to visit queen Victoria, and if she rejected his gospel to hurl her from the throne. James J. Strang contended for the place of Seer, and showed letters over the deceased prophet's signature, assuring him that he should be the successor in the event of Joseph's death. But the college of the Twelve had other views, and a vote on the subject. They declared that definite instructions, and the last will and testament of Joseph, had been delivered to them in secret council. It revoked all former designations and devolved the choice upon them.

Under the management of their sagacious chief, they elected the Peter of the Apostles, Brigham Young, to the responsible station.

This man, with a mien of the most retiring modesty and diffidence in ordinary intercourse in society, holds a spirit of ardent feeling and great shrewdness; and when roused in debate, or upon the preacher's stand, exhibits a boldness of speech and grasp of thought that awes and enchains with intense interest—controlling, soothing, or exasperating, at pleasure, the multitudes that listen to his eloquence. His title among the Saints is, "The lion of the Lord."

This enthronement drove Rigdon with a party to Pennsylvania, where in a short time his influence vanished and the band dispersed. Strang founded a city on the prairies of Wisconsin and had a numerous colony — he ultimately removed to Beaver island, in Michigan lake, and assumed the title of King of the Saints, where the small kingdom still exists. These bodies and their leaders were excommunicated by the great majority under the proper Seer — as was also William Smith, another competitor for the throne, and a party in Texas headed by Lyman White.

CHAPTER VI.

THE EXPULSION FROM NAUVOO.

WE have one more sad and fearful tale to tell about the Mormons ere their fortunes brightened. The mobocratic spirit did not expire when it destroyed the great leader. Threats and demonstrations clearly proved, that their present abode, which had been made lovely by unheard-of exertions, must be abandoned. The monster conflagrations on Green Plains cast a funereal glare on the spires of Nauvoo. The present venerable patriarch, uncle of the prophet Joseph, in prophetic vision announced that the whole people must retire to the wilderness, to grow into a multitude aloof from the haunts of civilization.

This matter was taken into consideration by Brigham and high council. The result was, that they would move as fast as possible across Iowa to the Missouri, and into the Indian country in the vicinity of Council Bluffs. Speculators flocked in, and offered nominal prices for what they significantly hinted would very soon be taken for nothing, if the offers were rejected. Houses, lots, and such goods as could not be moved, were sold by many in the fall of '44 and winter of '45; and several parties set out on the dreary journey early the following spring. Ox-carts and mule teams, loaded with all sorts of furniture, intermingled with women and children, wended their way slowly along on miry tracks, and crossed the swollen streams — fuel and grass scanty — but the spirits of all unbroken, save the sick and helpless. Closely bound together by common dangers and a common faith, they performed with alacrity their duties, and sympathy made the dreary journey one of social life. Their mirthfulness would be excited by little incidents, and even misfortunes were turned into jokes, as helping hands lent their aid to right a broken wheel or upset wagon. At the halting places, the spinning-wheel would be taken down and yarn spun to keep the knitting-needles going when riding during the day — and cloth made from wool sheared after the journey begun. At some places land was broken up and planted with seed, and a family or two left to rear a crop for those who were to follow in autumn. The lowing herd accompanied, and the milch kine yielded the nourishing beverage, and butter was made by the jolting of the wagons as they travelled along.

Still, the work continued unabated on the temple, for they were commanded to dedicate it before leaving the city of Beauty. It was the work of their hearts; each person owned a share of the noble pile, for his hands had labored on it, his tithes were expended there, and the ladies had contributed their ornaments to forward the sacred edifice. The mob became impatient of delay, and would not believe the Mormons sincere in the stipulated move. As the corn-fields began to ripen, the rabble collected, it is said, to the number of two thousand, and there were only three hundred of the old legion to defend the place against them. For three days an irregular fight went on, the assailants taking advantage of the high waving corn to conceal their approaches. The defenders nobly stood their ground, and drove them back at all points, and obtained a truce until spring; and then set diligently to work to complete the architectural ornaments, the holy emblems, and the angel on the lofty spire with his gospel. trump, to prepare the sacred temple for the last act assigned them by "revelation."*

When completed in all its minutiæ, the consecrators were called. From the surrounding country, and from parties far advanced on their prophetic journey, priests, elders, and bishops stole into the city as dusty travellers, and were suddenly metamorphosed to dignity by their robes of office; and one day, from

---

* I am informed by Captain S. Eastman, the accomplished scholar and artist, that the angel and trump are in Barnum's Museum, New York city.

high noon to the shade of night, was there a scene of rejoicing and solemn consecration of the beautiful edifice, on which so much anxiety and thought had lately been expended. There stood the Mormon temple in simple beauty, the pride of the valley. The great altar hung with festoons of flowers and green wreaths; the baptistic laver resting on twelve elaborately carved oxen, decorated with the symbolic glories, celestial, telestial, and terrestrial; the chaunt was sung, the prayers offered up, and the noble building, resplendent with lights of lamp and torches, solemnly dedicated to their own God. This done, and the walls were dismantled of ornaments and the symbols of their faith, the key-words of the mysteries, and lettered insignia were all removed with haste, except the sun, moon, and stars, carved in stones of the walls, and the temple forsaken, to be "profaned and trodden down by the Gentiles." A few brief hours were given to this brilliant pageant, and during this festive, joyous scene, a spectator would have supposed the actors expected that house to be their own for ever. There is something truly affecting in the contemplation of that devotional offering of so fine a temple, and then leaving it unscathed to the hand of their enemies.

From this time all defence ceased, and their enemies rested satisfied that the Mormons had decided to sell their possessions. Arrangements for surrender and departure were quickly made. Company after company followed the pioneers to the white Missouri; and many, crossing over in early summer, turned up the rich, but pestilential prairie sod, to prepare a harvest for autumn, and await the last of the trains. During that summer the plague and fever raged violently, and its ravages in the great bottom, on Indian and white men, were fearful. Winter approached — the tent and wagon body, with its hooped canvas, was exchanged for caves dug in the sides of the hills, and covered with logs, reeds, or cloth. The scanty fuel gave but little warmth to ward off the cold, made more searching from the piercing winds that howled over the delta prairies of the Missouri and Nebraska. Then came the ague, the rheumatism, and the scurvy, the terrible concomitants of fatigue, exposure, and scanty fare. Numbers died, and were buried in the rich alluvion. Awful as was that winter and spring, a cheerful heart and countenance was on all sides—a revelation gave permission to dance, to sing, and enjoy the swelling music from the excellent band that accompanied all their journeys.

Let us revert to the summer. A city was laid out, and soon the streets were dusty with the tread of busy industry. A printing-press issued the Frontier Guardian, the able exponent of their doctrines still. The name assumed was *Kane*, in honor of their guest and eloquent defender, whose historical oration on these dark periods of their fortunes, does equal honor to his charitable heart and intelligence—a sketch, however, of the epic kind, replete with poetical ornament and fervor.

It was at this time, in July, that a battalion of 520 men was recruited among them for the Mexican war. The government, knowing their intention to settle in California, would thus do them a favor by bearing a part of the expense of removal, test and demonstrate their fidelity, and show the reports of their enemies, concerning leagues with the Indians, to be false. The people, however, thought this only another persecution, yet submitted, to prove their patriotism. Enfeebled by disease, and scattered, it was an enormous effort. The elders called the congregation, and asked for recruits. The unmarried were *ordered* to *volunteer*—then fathers and husbands were called to leave their families, and the elders declared, if necessary, they would shoulder the musket. In three days the battalion was organized, and a merry ball, from "noon to dewy eve," was given, in holiday attire, by young men and maidens, joined in by reverend priests and matrons. The warriors were blessed in holy convocation, a prophecy made that they should conquer the country without a drop of blood shed in battle; and the battalion departed "in the name of the Lord."

Men were sent to the mountains, to the heads of the Missouri branches, and to California, to spy out the land, and the Calebs and Joshuas brought such a report of the Great Salt Lake Valley, that it was chosen for another "everlasting abode."

In the spring of 1847, a pioneer party of 143 men proceeded to open the way; and the host, in parties of tens, fifties, and hundreds, followed. This was an admirable system, and baffled the thievish desire of the Sioux, Crows, and Shoshones. A captain was over each division, but the captains of hundreds had the supervision of the smaller bands. A strict discipline of guard and march was observed. But the drain of the battalion threw the burden of toil much upon the women. Females drove teams of several yoke of oxen a thousand miles. A man could take three teams by the help of a woman and lad — he driving the middle one, and stepping forward to assist over the creeks with the foremost, and then bring up the rear ones — and at the camps unyoke and "hitch up" for his feebler coadjutors. Thus they wound along their weary way, at ten and fifteen miles a day — forded, or bridged, and ferried over, the Loup, the Horn, and Platte rivers on the plains, and the swollen streams of the Bear, and rushing Weber, in the mountains.

The first glimpse of the great valley on the road was from the summit of the second mountain, sixteen miles distant. As each team rose upon the narrow table, the delighted pilgrims saw the white salt beach of the Great Lake glistening in the never-clouded sunbeam of summer — and the view down the open gorge of the mountains, divided by a single conical peak, into the long-toiled-for vale of repose, was most ravishing to the beholders. Few such ecstatic moments are vouchsafed to mortals in the pilgrimage of life, when the dreary past is all forgotten, and the soul revels in unalloyed enjoyment, anticipating the fruition of hope. A few moments are allotted to each little party to gaze, to admire and to praise — and they begin to descend a steep declivity, amid the shades of a dense poplar grove, and for twenty-four hours are desiring to renew their pleasurable sensations on emerging from the frowning kanyon into the paradisaical valley, and long-sought-for home.

The journey was ended, but this gave no repose — industry continued. In five days a field was consecrated, fenced, ploughed, and planted, and seeds were germinating in the moisture of irrigating streams and the genial warmth of the internal heat of the earth, here brought to their notice by the thermal waters gushing from a thousand springs.

Though cramped in their means, and feeble as they were, nothing of interest on that long journey was left unobserved or unrecorded. Parties were directed to scour the vicinity of the road, and report on springs, timber, grass, and other objects of interest. An ingenious and accurate road-measurer was attached to a wagon, and a person designated to note the distances from point to point, and every feasible camping-ground was marked down — and a Directory for every rod of the road, admirably arranged and filled with useful information, was published for the use of those who should follow. The self-taught mathematician and learned apostle Orson Pratt, noted for latitude and longitude. The valley of the Platte is found to be almost an unbroken plane, whose slope is so gentle that the eye detects neither ascent nor descent, and from the Black Hills to its mouth is almost a straight line, and is perhaps the most remarkable trace, and finest natural road, in the world. The flat, or bottom, begins to spread at the hills, gradually from a point to ten or fifteen miles in width; and lies between bluffs, whose height is the origand plane or surface, out of which the river has excavated its valley. Few clumps of trees are along the banks; but the islands, secure from the prairie fires, are covered with groves of cottonwood. Irrigation would make valuable the level meadows, and to the north and south, pastures can be found covered with nutritious grasses, whose limits would be the range of the shepherds from the watering river.

Portions of the Platte have the appearance of shallow lakes, two or three miles wide; and in summer the stream is divided into thousands of currents by the sand islands. Its volume increases as you ascend toward its sources; the absorption by the soil and rapid evaporation on so wide a surface diminish the flow, while but few tributaries enter below the Sweetwater. What is here said of this river applies to the mountain streams generally; they attain their full size where the rivulets are collected into one at the mountain base, and, in many instances, disappear in the sands of the plains far distant from the ocean.

Near the Sweetwater, they discovered a lake with a deposition of borax, and another with an abundance of soda, which they named "Saleratus Lake," and where they loaded up a few years' supply of the alkali, to use in its native state in preparing biscuit and bread. They noted the beds of bituminous coal on the Platte, and in the Green river basin — the petroleum issuing with the springs near Bear river, and tested the poisonous quality of other fountains, leaving a warning to the traveller not to suffer his cattle to drink at them. The beds of gypsum, the character of the soil, the minerals and geology of the route, were not neglected in that journal; and the elevations of the summits on the road were barometrically taken. Thus observant and industrious, they press on, and emerge cheerfully into the valley of the Great Salt Lake.

The pioneers arrived on the 21st of July, and the Church Presidency on the 24th, which latter day is their grand epoch, which, in the language of the third one in rank, of that corps, on the third anniversary,—"is the day whose events are of the most importance to mankind of any that ever transpired, the creation of Adam and birth of Jesus Christ alone excepted."

And there they are, bidding defiance to their persecutors and ready to fight for the land that has been fertilized by their labors, and made valuable by their perseverance and almost superhuman exertions. It has been made sacred to them by the blood of their sons, which has flowed in its defence against hostile Indians. It is holy ground, set apart to their use by the rites of their conscience-loved religion. Nor could they be easily molested. It were more than a march to the ancient Aztec city, to carry an army to their mountain home. In those distant fastnesses they feel secure against any force the United States would send against them. But they invite no such attention as this, and seek to evade it; they will do all that conscience and a sense of right will allow, to avoid collision. They feel well entitled to the land, as already well paid for — and can but expect a grant for Improvements and Educational purposes like other new States which will cover all the lands that would be bought in the market. They also feel it due to them, to grant them the privilege of self-control; to exercise just laws over their own people, and of their faith, by persons of their own choice or recommendation, and that Gentile governors and judges are unjust impositions upon them.

They were driven to a land worthless and savage — left three years without protection or control — have formed their habits, agricultural, mechanical, and religious or moral; and know better than all the world what is suited to their condition. Non-interference with the vote of its citizens is the wish of Utah. True, they could be annoyed by cutting off supplies of luxuries, and blockading the routes by which they receive their poor emigrants, but that would at once make a foreign nation in the centre of American territory.

But to enjoy their own laws of a republican character, permitted and sanctioned by the Constitution, they are determined upon doing, and have the administration of them in their own way. Soon they may be numerous enough to demand the position of a sovereign State, and knock loudly for admission into the Union.

Their feeling toward the Union was significantly shown at the third celebration of their memorable epoch of arrival. A small part of its history may serve to illustrate.

At ten o'clock in the morning, the roaring cannon gave notice that the time of gathering to the Bowery on the temple block was at hand. The dignitaries of "The Church," and officers of the United States' exploring party were, by invitation, at the new edifice of the President, Brigham Young, where they were received with all the gentlemanly kindness and urbanity which distinguishes the governor of Utah. At eleven a large military escort, handsomely equipped, and commanded by General Wells, a hero in the three days' defence of Nauvoo, with a fine band of music, followed by twenty-four bishops in official robes, each holding a flag, filed in front of the mansion, and halted. The guests, dignitaries, and Presidency, were then arranged in procession, and all proceeded under conduct of the general, his aides, and Marshal of the Day — music playing, the banners waving, and the cannon at the Bowery resounding, to the forum, where the exercises were to be held. Here were assembled, in most perfect order and quiet, about six thousand persons — all in neat holiday attire, and pleasure beaming on every countenance. When the Orator, Presidency, Fathers, or "aged men," and principal guests were seated on the numerous benches of the pulpit stand an invocation of Heaven's blessing was made by one of the twelve.

Then followed the reading of the order of exercises by the Marshal, and the Orator proceeded to deliver his eloquent appeal to the pride, the patriotism, and sense of justice of the attentive listeners. He recounted their many trials and the glorious result; and called on them to uphold their honor and their rights against all invasion, and in their name declared an attack upon them for this, would be resisted. Speeches were made afterward by the President and others, all tending to rouse attention to the character of the celebration, and designate more pointedly why and for what cause they were there to commemorate the day.

Next came the pageant of the day, to which we call attention. It was the presentation to the governor of Deserét of the Constitution of the United States, and their own, for his and his successors' guardian care. The presentation of the Constitution was made by twenty-four "aged fathers," silver-headed men, sons and descendants of '76. In a neat, brief speech, their foreman admonished the governor that those fathers before him were soon to leave the scene enacting on life's busy stage; and before they went, no more to return, while the present civil governments were in being, they desired to place in charge the legacy they had received from the past generation, to be transmitted on intact to the future, till the consummation of time. This was the glorious and divine Constitution, that had been given by inspiration of God to the statesmen of an earlier day—and this they asked should be placed among the archives of their growing state as a holy treasure, and to be regarded "as the palladium of our liberty," and the supreme ruler under God, that sits over the destinies of the United States; an unembodied power, existing solely in the love and faith of its *subject freemen.* And it must be held sacred, and every person in the mountains was called to enrol himself its sworn defender; for portentous clouds are rolling up the eastern sky, and the original supporters are soon to break allegiance to the silent but eloquent constitution, and, insensate by the will of Heaven, will rush to imbrue their hands in fraternal blood — while aloof, the chosen depositaries shall cherish the holy casket, and descend at last like the eagle from its eyrie, to carry back to the repentant remnant that peace by which this highly favored land alone can prosper — and, along with the civil instrument, that truth which alone can make them free.

The festivities were continued by a sumptuous banquet at the Presidential mansion, given to those escorted to the Bowery, and after an informal return, toasts, music, songs, and jovial speeches were showered forth until evening, when the delighted multitude, without an incident to mar the harmony of the occasion, dispersed; apparently believing that they were the greatest people on earth, and their rulers the wisest men in existence. They had been told by their Seer that they need not fear any earthly power; and that it was determined to maintain their identity as a State, whatever Congress or President at Washington should say or do, and the people one and all responded a hearty Amen, it shall be so, it is the fiat of justice and of Heaven. Subsequent events have proved that practically it is just as they have determined; a State they are, making their own local laws and enforcing them, whether under the name of Territory of Utah, or State of Deserét — they have made (and is it not just?) that territory into the "Land of the Honey Bee," and would fain call it their own

CHAPTER VII.

PROGRESS AT THE GREAT SALT LAKE.

THERE are a few items of Mormon belief and practice, and the subject of titles to land, to which it may not be amiss to refer. The first thing we notice is the "working of miracles" and curing instantly diseases. Claiming all the gifts vouchsafed to the early church, this performance of miracles becomes a necessary thing, and to their own minds is conclusively done. It is for confirming themselves in the truth, not to demonstrate to "those without," who seek after a sign, that the power is given. Evading poisons, and healing the sick, are the most usual. An eye-witness related to me the following. A mad dog rushed through the streets of the city, snapping at every animal it met, and bit a lad severely. The cattle all died. The Elders were immediately called to the bedside of the doomed boy. Parents, brothers, and relations stood dissolved in grief, awaiting anxiously the spasms and dissolution of the family pet. The chief priest commands silence — the voice of "mighty prayer" ascends in supplication — the consecrated oil is produced — the child is anointed — and the prayer of faith restores the son to his overjoyed parents.

Diseases are held to be demoniac possessions, and by casting out the devil, you can cure the afflicted. Professors in the healing art are of small account in the philosophy of the healthy, and medicines are forbidden by the Prophet, except to the weak in faith, who are permitted a "meagre diet and mild herbs." With inconsistent practice, many make use of the doctor and his drugs, however, and in reply to this, allege that they have not yet attained to a full measure of faith, but hope to improve till they can take up deadly things without injury; and assert that when by accident any Saint takes poison, he escapes harmless. Voluntary trials are "temptings of the Lords" and receive the proper penalty. The Seer teaches the duty of asking for the Elders' hands, — yet he is said to employ Gentile doctors to cure the "Ague Fiend," the hardest yet to deal with. This puzzles the faithful, but they get over it pretty well by saying, he has infirmities no doubt, and the devil is allowed to torment for any dereliction of duty — but as Seer, that does not affect him or his revelations.

The equally well-attested miracles of Mesmerism and Mona chism are admitted to be real — only that they are done by Beelzebub, who does it to deceive and make those recipients and disbursers of favor believe they have divine power. At the presentation of relics or manipulations, the evil spirit in the person is driven out by a stronger one; and after the wonder is over, returns with a sevenfold violence. Further, the Devil, mistrusting that this power was about to be given again, and angels sent to minister to the Saints, tried to forestall the effect and instructed his imps in the arts of miracle-working. He also gave visions to Swedenborg in order to throw discredit on the Spirit teachings of Moroni, and is now destroying the Mormon testimony in many places by what is called spiritual manifestations.

LABOR.

The dignity of labor is held sacred by the Mormons, and exemplified in their organization and requirements. A lazy person is either accursed or likely to be; usefulness is their motto; and those who will not keep themselves, or try their best, are left to starve into industry. This is inculcated in their creed, though the prophet Joseph was excused from physical labor at Kirtland, his attention being sufficiently occupied with the government. Every one is expected to work and bring in his tithes, and the president sets the example in the valley, by working at his trade of carpenter, on his own mills in the kanyon. It is a well-devised scheme, and the more flourishing the laborers, the greater is the income of the priests. This income is expended on public works, the temple, the bridges, and public charity, and support of the families of those on missionary duty.

The labor for support of oneself and family is taught to be of as divine a character, as public worship and prayer. In practice, their views unite them so as to procure all the benefits of social christianity without running into communism. The priest and the bishop make it their boast that, like Paul the tentmaker, they earn their bread by the sweat of the brow; and teach by example on the week-day, what they preach on the Sabbath, concerning the virtue of industry. On the pulpit stand they dispense the word of the gospel, and *work* harder than when they plant, sow, or reap in the field, or team for wood in the kanyon, or ply the spade, the trowel, or the hammer. This brings all orders together, and makes them acquainted where no art or concealment of feeling is practised, and destroys that distinction of pastor and layman by the difference of dress and demeanor, which keeps them strangers to each other's real sentiments. And it gives the priest the advantage of knowing the turns of thought, the doubts on doctrines, and degree of enlightenment of those who are to be his auditors, and he can adapt his discourse accordingly, and make an impression.

Priests are made without regard to their learning or acquaintance with books — and the object is gained of suiting every capacity; if a man finds his intellectual strength insufficient in one place, he must seek elsewhere for his sphere of action. They understand that apparent candor and simplicity in the propagandist, are more likely to attract the attention of the uncultivated mass than the finest parade of ability and scholarship. Many are ready to enter upon an argument with, or express their opinions before, one of their own calibre, but distrust the professional polemic, and attribute his success in a disputation to ingenious sophistry, and remain unconvinced when unable to reply. Hence the frequent disclaimer of Mormons, of learning and rhetoric, and reliance on the "moving of the spirit"— interior teachings, the commands of God, and sense of duty, are the alleged springs of their mission. Thus Forsden, last year in Sweden, began his preaching by laying hands on his brother who was ill, and thus curing him, attracted attention from the neighbors. To these he related in his simple manner, the story of the Prophet in the West, and restoration of miraculous gifts to saints. Curiosity was excited among a few peasants, and the news spread over the city; then he harangued at the street-corners, which caused his arrest by the magistrate and a reprimand. He repeated his preaching, and was again taken up and fined and ordered to cease his heretical work; but meekly replied that he simply preached Christ crucified, and being commanded of God to do it, must obey him rather than man. Spectators were moved by his simple submission to such views of higher law at the risk of imprisonment or of life. Punished, he glorified his Lord aloud in praise and song, for being worthy to suffer, and was finally taken forcibly across the channel to Denmark, but left several disciples to spread his doctrines.

Involuntary labor by negroes is recognised by custom; those holding slaves, keep them as part of their family, as they would wives, without any law on the subject. Negro caste springs naturally from their doctrine of blacks being ineligible to the priesthood.

PROSELYTING.

The Mormon missionaries address the cupidity, as well as the religious hopes and fears of those they address. Travelling from city to city, calling at the houses, and talking to those on the wayside familiarly, and working occasionally at some trade for support, they stealthily introduce the subject at heart, and take many unawares. It is usual to use the Socratic method, and ask if the former church had not gifts, if there were not promised "signs following," and if any church now shows them—then they follow up by exposition of their doctrines, and claim at the Zion of America to have all the promises. If the listener is not a man of wealth, he will be told that the command is to gather to the mountains, where the finest land is offered for a few shillings, just enough to pay for surveying and recording a title to a farm. To the peasantry of Europe this is a powerful, an irresistible argument. Accustomed to see the aristocracy owners of the soil, they yearn to call a parcel of ground their own, for it conveys a feeling of translation from serfdom to princedom; and perhaps such make the firmest patriots in this new empire. And the doctrine of every woman a husband, every Magdalen pure when baptised, will secure many of the softer sex; so that we may not be surprised at the sudden conversion of whole families, and tens of thousands, as the popular eloquence falls on the ears of those who emerge from factories, workshops, and collieries. Glad news to such is the command to go to the mountains, where they become lords of the soil; and, by a simple declaration, can be aided thither from the "perpetual charity fund," which is liberally supplied by the happy ones already at the land of promise. The assertion of the president of the stake in England may well be credited, who says that thirty-five thousand are enrolled in the Liverpool "stake," and ready to come over, but not one tenth have the means to reach the mountains. Three hundred thousand are the estimated Mormons in England and Wales. Zealous beyond measure to proselyte, trusting to further instruction when they return with their converts, to the teachers, whose official dignity carries a prestige of authority, the street preachers "cry aloud and spare not," baptize by scores all who express a willingness to be called by "that name" in which they glory. Many come back with lungs exhausted and health impaired by such exertions, and often will they point out to you the passer-by, and say "that is the holy man who exhausted his strength by preaching in the open air in London, this word of the Latter Days"—or the hero of a missionary army in some part of the world.

THEIR LAND TITLES.

They issue a right of occupancy from the State Register's office. This is contingent on the grant of the general government, of course, and forms one of the subjects on which they may come into collision with the supreme authority. They will not, without protest, buy the land, and hope that grants will be made to actual settlers or the State, sufficient to cover their improvements. If not, the State will be obliged to buy, and then confirm the titles already given.

In the extensive territory of Utah, probably not one acre in ten thousand is fit for profitable cultivation, and only the fertile strips will recompense the surveying. The immense pasturage around cultivable spots will be fed in common, and of course never purchased by individuals.

When the Mormons arrived in the valley, they did not quarrel about the fertile, eligible plats, but put a portion under cultivation jointly, and made equitable distribution of the proceeds of the crop, according to wants, labor, and seed bestowed. The city was laid off into lots and numbered; and by mutual consent they were assigned by the Presidency, who selected according to their judgment, placing those in the vicinity that they wished for good neighborhood, and allotting off the balance. Each individual paid a small sum to meet the expense of surveying and recording. A section on the south of the city, six miles square, called the "Big Field," was fenced at public cost, and divided up into five acre lots, with convenient lanes between, and those who would actually work them, were allowed to choose, or receive by lot, from one to eight of these. A Poor Farm of forty acres is in the centre, controlled by the bishops. All lines of division and boundary are run with the cardinal points. The present limits of farms will doubtless be recognised, though the United States' surveys should make different boundaries: by purchase in a tract by the State, or from a common fund, individuals will be secured in their *vested rights.* When the lands are offered in the market, public sentiment will allow no bidders against the Presidency.

After the assignments were made, persons commenced the usual speculations of selling according to eligibility of situation. This called out anathemas from the spiritual power, and no one was permitted to traffic for fancy profit: if any sales were to be made, the first cost and actual value of improvements were all that was to be allowed. All speculative sales are made sub rosa. Exchanges are made, and the records kept by the Register. The land belongs to the Lord, and his Saints are to use so much as each can work profitably.

We must not forget that these occupants hold themselves the Lord's stewards, who are bound to look after his interest, by making any unfruitful portion of the heritage produce food for his saints — and, having found a waste tract unoccupied as it should be, (for the miserable Utahs are of no account on this supposition) and imparted to it by the actual labor of their sinews all its present value, it is doubly theirs, by right divine and subjugation. And truly they have a claim by conquest from the roving Indians. They first settled on the war-grounds of Snake-Diggers and Utahs, interposing between belligerents. Wars are waged continually between the bands or sub-tribes, which, with disease, is fast destroying them. But when the Mormons extended north and south, they encroached on hunting and fishing grounds, and the usual winter camping places, and scared off the game. The Shoshones have consulted discretion, and, though threatening attack, have "kept the peace." Not so the Utahs. In the winter of 1849 they became insolent in Utah Valley, killed cattle and boasted of it, entered houses and frightened women and children, took provisions forcibly, and compelled those on the farms to retire within the fort. Complaints of these things were sent to head-quarters, and after all peaceable overtures were disregarded, the Utah war was resolved upon.

Two companies from the City of Salt Lake joined the forces in Utah valley, and proceeded to attack the quarters of the Indians. The latter were well posted in the dry channels of the Timpanogos, and screened by a cottonwood forest and thick willow clumps, but were finally driven out by the cannon and rifles at long shots, after three days' skirmishing. The soldiers retired every night to the fort, a mile distant from the battle-field. One young man of the assailants was killed. The Indians decamped the third night for the mountain kanyons, now filled with snow; and the measles being among them, the exposure killed many. "Old Elk," the terror of the mountains, was found dead on the trail. He had long boasted that no single person or trapper could live with him in the valleys, and numbers are supposed to have fallen under his rifle. A party was driven up Table Mountain, but were induced to come down and surrender. They were guarded in camp until the morning, and then ordered to give up their weapons. They refused to do this, and acting in a sullen and hostile manner, were fired upon and nearly all killed immediately. A few broke through the line of sentinels and endeavored to escape by crossing the lake on the ice, but were chased down by horsemen and "ceased to breathe." My informant was an actor in the terrible scene, and seemed disposed to paint it in as soft colors as possible. A like chastisement was given the year previous to a small band of Shoshones, and a second has since been inflicted on the Utahs, and the chief, Patsowits, caught and killed by the bowstring; and this thorough work makes such an impression on them that they will fear to offend, which is the humane policy. Had public sentiment sanctioned a similar policy with the Seminoles, what sacrifices of blood and treasure would have been avoided!

About forty were killed by powder and measles; and the band of old "Stick-in-the-head," a chief of note, was so thinned that they immediately begged for peace. A large number of prisoners were taken, mostly women and children, carried into Fort Utah, and lodged under the cannon platform in tents until they could be distributed among the families in the valley. They were fed bounteously on beef, and it was a sight for a painter to see this motley group feast on the generosity of the capturers. Squaws and children were generously taken into the houses, and the trial made to teach them domestic service. But it was a failure: they soon deserted the *comforts* of the white man's house for the snowy home of the kanyons.

It is a curious matter of reflection, that those whose *mission* it is to convert these aborigines by the sword of the spirit, should thus be obliged to destroy them — but they stoutly affirm that these people will yet, under their instruction, fulfil the prophecy that "a nation shall be born in a day;" and when they have completed the destined time, will listen to the truth and become "a fair and delightsome people."

THE UTAHS.

This tribe consists of several bands under different chieftains, united by a common language and affinities as well as by numerous intermarriages. They range over a large region of country, extending from California to New Mexico. They are a superstitious race, and have many cruel customs. Some tribes are reputed good warriors.

In the vicinity of the Salt Mountain in Youab Valley is a remarkable well or circular pit, at the bottom of which is a spring of water which rises a few feet and finds an outlet in the loose strata. It is called by the Utahs, Pun-gun. They fancy in this resides a child, that comes to the surface at the setting of the sun; and when one approaches, it cries and screams for help, making most frightful contortions; but should any attempt to aid the child to escape, they would be carried to the lower regions. It is the ghost cave of the Indians, and in it is the Blue Beard of the squaws which frightens into obedience unruly pappooses. Near this spot occurred a tragedy which may exemplify their religious notions. The witness of the scene thus relates it. He was travelling the trail, and seeing a village of the Utah, he turned toward it for curiosity and trade. Passing among the lodges, he heard a low wail within one of the wigwams. He stopped before it, and presently a lad of fourteen years apparently, came out sobbing bitterly, and sat down, placing his face in his hands and resting them upon his knees. Several Indians collected about the place, and in silence appeared to be waiting for some event of importance. He heard a sound like that of loading a rifle within the lodge. An exclamation of satisfaction escaped from a robust brave, as he emerged from the narrow entrance, as though he was now sure of accomplishing some desirable object of long contemplation.

The boy sprang up with a piteous shriek at the sound, then as if resigned to his fate, he cast one lingering look at the snow-capt hills — then dropping his head, closed his eyes to the light of day, and was shot through the heart by the unrelenting savage.

On inquiry, the trader was told that this boy was a prisoner, taken long since from a neighboring tribe, and that he was sent off to take care of his master, who had that morning died. Such prisoners they keep to accompany the deceased to the happy hunting-grounds in the spirit world.

When they have no captives, if a person of note dies, and a stranger is with them, the rights of hospitality are disregarded, and the visitor must be sacrificed to the manes of the departed. This requires the trading bands to be vigilant and in force; for should a runner come in with the news of any killed in battle with their enemies, the most friendly feelings would be instantly converted into those of destruction, to satisfy their religious custom. When a chief dies, his lodge is burned, the horses and dogs are killed, and all his arms and cooking utensils are buried with him. Burial-places are sought high up the kanyons, usually in clefts of rock; and boulders are heaped around, leaving a small opening, into which food is thrust for several weeks after the sepulture.

Chieftainship descends from father to son. A late chief, acting on the plurality law, left above thirty sons, most of whom have small clans under them. His true successor is a fine brave Indian, with the largest band immediately around him; and he exercises control over all when he chooses. He is a friend of the Mormons. A half-brother of his, named Walker, has become rich and celebrated for his success in stealing horses from the Mexicans. He has a large drove of cattle, with many followers. He lately located near the San Pete settlement, and professed a strong desire to learn agriculture from his civilized neighbors, and promised conformity on the part of his band. This is the man who, regarded in the mountains as a petty adventurer, has often been so romantically eulogised in the States, and furnishes a theme of praise among the Mormons, being esteemed a trophy to the power of their religion, a kind of first-fruits of their policy. But ere this he may have resumed his robber habits, and frustrated the intention of his Mormon friends of making him the head chief of the tribe.

The different tribes of the Utahs are frequently at war with each other, and they have an eternal national war with the Shoshones The Mormon settlements partially interpose between the twc great tribes, exerting an influence upon both, and ensuring them a controlling power ultimately. But the most eligible position for a commanding influence over the mountain tribes, is to be chosen in the Green River Basin, either on Black's Fork, where Fort Bridger is built, for a defensive trading post, or on the Colorado or branches. It could control and aid the emigrant travel to Oregon and California, as the routes must fork in that section. The Snakes or Shoshones, estimated at several thousands, are on the north. The Crows are to the north-east. This band numbers eight hundred lodges, and is under the most military and severe training. A principal chief governs despotically. He has a council of ten, which is convened every night to relate the occurrences of the day, and give plans for the morrow. On the march no one is permitted to leave the ranks without the signal of the chief. When camp is to be made, the chief, who is always two hundred yards in advance, halts and throws down his horse-trappings, and no one is to come nearer "his medicine" than a prescribed distance, without call. His lodge is set up by the squaws, and others then encircle it. Death is the penalty of disobedience. Sub-parties are sent off for plunder, under similar discipline. The Sioux tribe is on the east of the basin; the Oglallahs, or Cheyennes, to the south-east, and the universal Utahs to the south, all of which need no further description.

A fort and Indian agency, on this neutral or war-ground of all these tribes, would communicate with each. All their plans could easily be discovered. They could be played off against each other, and advantage taken of their animosities. If a humane policy is the proper one, then here is the place for a pacificator, and the interposition of good offices to prevent their internecine contests. And no more influential person could be found in an agency there, than the enterprising man already connected with them by marriage and habit, and who now resides as a trader at Fort Bridger.

The builder of Fort Bridger is one of the hardy race of mountain trappers who are now disappearing from the continent, being enclosed in the wave of civilization. These trappers have made a thousand fortunes for eastern men, and by their improvidence have nothing for themselves. Major Bridger, or "old Jim," has been more wise of late, and laid aside a competence; but the mountain tastes, fostered by twenty-eight years of exciting scenes, will probably keep him there for life. He has been very active, and traversed the region from the head-waters of the Missouri to the Del Norte — and along the Gila to the Gulf, and thence throughout Oregon and the interior of California. His graphic sketches are delightful romances. With a buffalo-skin and piece of charcoal, he will map out any portion of this immense region, and delineate mountains, streams, and the circular valleys called "holes," with wonderful accuracy; at least we may so speak of that portion we traversed after his descriptions were given. He gives a picture, most romantic and enticing, of the head-waters of the Yellow Stone. A lake sixty miles long, cold and pellucid, lies embosomed amid high precipitous mountains. On the west side is a sloping plain several miles wide, with clumps of trees and groves of pine. The ground resounds to the tread of horses. Geysers spout up seventy feet high, with a terrific hissing noise, at regular intervals. Waterfalls are sparkling, leaping, and thundering down the precipices, and collect in the pool below. The river issues from this lake, and for fifteen miles roars through the perpendicular kanyon at the outlet. In this section are the Great Springs, so hot that meat is readily cooked in them, and as they descend on the successive terraces, afford at length delightful baths. On the other side is an acid spring, which gushes out in a river torrent; and below is a cave which supplies "vermilion" for the savages in abundance. Bear, elk, deer, wolf, and fox, are among the sporting game, and the feathered tribe yields its share for variety, on the sportsman's table of rock or turf.

Another region he visited and trapped in, lies to the west of the Del Norte, and north of the Gila. This he represents as once the abode of man, where there are gigantic ruins of masonry, which he describes with the clearness of a Stephens. Trees have grown over these destroyed towns, and fruits and nuts load their branches; and among the animals are the wild boar and grizzly bear. His own words are: "this fertile place is large enough for three States, and is the most delightful spot that ever God made for man." As a guide for explorers the services of that man would be invaluable.

The public attention has been called in Missouri to the feasible line of road from Western Missouri to the Great Valley—and where the proper track for the Pacific Railway may be found if built from the Missouri river near Independence. This route would take the line of the Kanzas, up the Republican fork and across to the South Platte, and thence along the Lodge Pole Creek to the south terminus of the Black Hills, where they would be turned; and then across the rich Laramie plains, leaving the Medicine-Bow Mountains on the south, and crossing the North Platte into the South Pass, over the Coal Basin, skirting the Bear River Mountains at the northern base, near Bridger's Fort; and through the Bear and Weber Kanyons, which are represented by the mountain men as level and practicable, and confirmed by distant views as probably correct, issue upon the Kamas prairie to the Timpanogos, and course down its banks to the Valley of Lake Utah.

It is not always reliable information which we gain from the mountain travellers; but, from the descriptions given me by them, the best route from Utah lies through the passes to Seveir Lake, and south-west to the depression in the Sierra Nevada north of Los Angeles, where the Tulare valleys are entered, and from which a port is to be selected on the Pacific. The Mormon settlements nearer the rim of the basin, may incline the road more south, and would not much increase the distance. This wonderfully level track across the country strikes the mind with surprise. One scarcely is conscious of a hill on the road, while the immense mountains are ever before and around him.

The difficulty this work will encounter lies in the accumulation of snow in the Weber and Timpanagos kanyons, during winter;

exploration and observation are required to settle its presumed practicability, and the amount of this impediment. Such a road, within our limits, would be the crowning work of the century and indeed of all antecedent time, so gigantic is it in its conceptions; and it would be so wonderful in its results on trade and the destinies of the race, that all other human efforts sink in insignificance before it. It would strike the centre of the great valley of the Mississippi, and the commerce and the travel that should come from Asia would there divide, to take its appropriate destination for the Gulf of Mexico or the St. Lawrence; or on the many lines of internal communication to the Atlantic seaboard.

CHAPTER VIII.

SELF-GOVERNMENT.

In concluding our notice of this new territory, and of its peculiar people, we may be allowed once more to advert especially to the subject of controlling the government of Deserét. We hear that officers sent to them have had their feelings so outraged by treasonable expressions toward the supreme government, that they have felt it obligatory to return and place the subject before the national legislature and the chief magistrate. This may have resulted from too hasty conclusions, and from not marking the qualifications usually due to such denunciations. Among portions of the citizens in every State, we may hear very opprobrious terms used. The government is frequently proclaimed corrupt, and dangerous to liberty, in party declamation; the writers and speakers being ready to defend it, however, with their life-blood.

We know that a prejudice existed against the appointment of one, at least, who went to Utah in an official capacity; and the Mormons were prepared to receive him with distrust, politically and morally; and however unjust the prejudice, it undoubtedly had its bad influence — and in attacking one with harsh language, the cause may have become common to all.

Now, the Mormons regard themselves as placed in the position of our colonial fathers; with this difference, that the latter felt the burden of taxation without representation; the Mormons, an injustice in enforcing law upon them by *foreigners.* They have formed every thing on the model of a republican State; adopted a constitution, liberal, free, and tolerant of conscience in religion; and have a criminal code which applies to their peculiar situation and feelings. It is not to be presumed that lawyers, though eminent at home, fresh from crowded cities, and long drilled in municipal laws suited to old societies, can have a just appreciation of the statutes of this wild country, which have a peculiar religious sanction from the dependence of the civil code on *revelation.* Nor will the community place the same confidence in such judges, as in those whose acquaintance with their views and opinions is a matter of experience; and whose interests and sympathies are bound up together. And, too, we must remember that it is a matter of conscience to bring all subjects of contention before the heads of their own family, the household of the church.

So long, therefore, as they demean themselves as good industrious citizens of the United States, being geographically separate from other society, with no admiralty causes to adjudicate, and pay their portion of the indirect taxation for the support of the government, they feel a right to demand confidence enough to be allowed to have persons resident among themselves appointed to administer the laws over them, and fill official stations. And they can well laugh at all attempts to control them otherwise, though they may submit in appearance, to prevent collision.

And then comes up the question, is not this after all a matter of political etiquette? and is it wise to make a case of treason on such a point? They acknowledge the binding force of the Constitution, claim to be American citizens, and also to have a right that this courtesy be allowed them, after so many privations and sufferings endured, to make the wilderness and desert a habitable abode. To enforce rulers over them from abroad, by the power of the bayonet, will entail perpetual war, or necessitate the raising a force, and making an expenditure of funds such as has never been called for at one time since our national existence. The theatre of war would be at a great distance, and all supplies must be transported a thousand miles on land carriage. And what would be gained in the end? Nothing but the same as persecution has heretofore given, increase of Mormon power. Indeed we are not sure but the leaders would like a display of force, in order to raise the cry of persecution, and turn the attention of the people upon foreign objects.

But we must remember that this is no insurrection of a part of a State: the population is a unit, engaged to a man in the sacred cause of their freedom to govern themselves. They must be convinced of error, before they can abandon their position without disgrace. And it will be a difficult thing to bring one portion of American citizens to fight against another on such an issue. The Herald at once proclaims that liberty of conscience is infringed. They will be considered as contending for the right to worship God in their own way, and to govern themselves as other States do. Separated by a three months' journey from other organized communities, they are harmless to them, and individuals must seek molestation, if they have aught to complain about. Why then, they will ask, peril life and treasure, when the issue can be evaded so easily, and the benefits of their position as a State secured to the country, by means which it is generous to adopt, and in our power to grant?

The principle involved is the right of sovereignty; this is already conceded, so far as it can be, to the general government, and soon a half million of persons will demand the true position of a State, or declare themselves independent of all. Surely this looks like the case in contemplation of the wise man, when he advised so prudently, "leave off contention before it is meddled with," which can be applied to governments, as well as to individuals.

Smarting under a bitter recollection of violence, that people could easily be goaded into rebellion, or rather into a warfare. A small force would be a vain insult among them. Protection they ask not, nor do they need it. They are a mighty moral force among the threatening cloud of savages on our frontiers. They compel the Indian to respect them. But they would dread far more than this the contaminating influence of an idle soldiery among them, upon industry,—yet more than all, the gallantry of the epaulettes upon their peculiar institution of polygamy. A jealousy would be provoked that would be "cruel as the grave."

The whole United States army would probably be insufficient to garrison and control a hostile population on a line of five hundred miles, and enforce civil law by foreign judges. It could only compel martial law to be acquiesced in, if once such a force were well quartered upon them.

INTERNAL DISCORD.

The causes which are at work to break up the clanship and oneness of the Mormon State, and reduce that people to the situation of others, with various beliefs and interests, are among themselves. The bursting power is internal, and loosening the outward bands will discover it. In short, the true policy is apparent, and may be given in their own peculiar phrase, "let them severely alone;" which they apply to Gentile rulers sent to control their movements.

The first disturbing element we notice is the introduction of polygamy; and yet they give, or profess to allow, all the freedom to the females that is found in any Christian nation. Their education is quite as free and liberal as to the other sex, thus far. But with all this do we find them advocating the inferiority of woman in dignity of station. "Gentile gallantry and fashion" is declared to have reversed the natural relationship and social position of the sexes; and that to give the post of honor or of comfort to the lady, is absurd. If there is but one seat, they say it of right belongs to the gentleman, and it is the duty and place of a man to lead the way, and let the fair partner enter the house or room behind him. The glory of a woman is constantly held forth to be a "mother in Israel," or, literally, a child-tender. The delicate sentiment of companionable qualities and mental attachments finds no place in the philosophy of plurality of wives, separate from grosser sensuous enjoyments. While introducing this great cause of disruption and jealousies into families, they cultivate in schools the arts of peace that tend to soften and elevate a community; and the antagonistic principles, one of rolling back to Asiatic stationary civilization, the other of progressive enlightenment, must come into collision. What then is the effect of their law of plurality? The sacred bond between two persons, by which the twain are one, as declared in Holy Writ, is desecrated. In that union of the wills, the affections, and interests, lies the hope of improvement of the condition of society; and by the laws of nature and of grace, there the peace of the world and realization of the Christian's hopes are centred. The law establishing the family circle was the first promulgated in social relations. And again the sacred historian takes up the theme, and relates the full-souled offering of his heart by Adam, and acknowledgment of equality and sameness; and then he declares that for this cause a man shall forsake all other ties, to obey the sacred promptings of a guileless nature, in conjugal fidelity to one wife — which became the law of grace, and four thousand years after was once more affirmed as the holy rule of the sexes, by the Lord of all.

Nor is this a subject ever to be lightly touched, for he is a traitor to his country, to humanity, and to himself, who can point the finger of scorn, or lessen in the minds of any, the sacredness of the dual marriage; and, as all are scholars, from the cradle to the grave, as well as teachers in the social world, let every rightly balanced mind exert itself to learn, and to picture the delights and the sorrows of *home*, on the truthful basis of their heaven-born origin. When the lofty genius of the poet rises highest in scenes that enrapture and gladden less gifted minds, what inspires but this spirit of love—when the statesman is tossing restlessly on the waves of ambition, or the warrior rides fearless on the heights of a thousand dangers, their souls are nerved to their tasks by the rewards of love's admiration; and the peace of the Christian nestles in the heart, and bids each pure soul cherish, in calm sublimity, the love of its nearest and dearest neighbor; and all turn for beauty of expression and truthful illustration of the social good, to the appropriate comparison of "the love of woman." Let nothing then come between the object of regard and the whole affections — but rather call in aid every thing that can strengthen the union of souls, and bring it to perfection.

To offer the person for a companion, and withhold the affections, would be like the Siamese twins in the death of Chang, while

Eng should live, a body attached to, but not of him—it would be the embrace of a corpse, galvanized into some of the motions of life; but the warmth, the virtue of the vital principle, departed for ever. And this must soon become the social fate of our mountain brethren, unless a change comes over the spirit of their revelations, and they return to the primitive law of the marriage relation.

EFFECT OF PLURALITY ON THE YOUNG.

A second consideration, arising from the same cause, is in the relation of parents and children. Separated now from those who can persecute them, it is hard to keep up the enthusiasm of the mass, by reference to the persecutions heretofore endured. But to the young, the children of the mountains, these are "oft-told tales," jejune and tiresome. The youth there are no fanatics, and seem to care but little for the detail of doctrines.

And the contemplation of plurality is highly distasteful to the young ladies of any independence of feeling, however acquiesced in by the more advanced in age. The subject was placed before one in its practical light, and the reply was most decided and prompt against such an arrangement. Asked if she could consent to become Mrs. Blank, No. 20, or No. 40 — or if now in youthful life she was espoused to one of her choice, and who was all the world to her; and then, though ranking No. 1, when the first blush of beauty had departed, she could be contented to have the husband call at her domicil after several weeks' absence and say, "I am really glad to see you dearest, and how delighted it would make me to spend an hour here, but — and, by the way, have you seen my last bride No. 17; how sweet a girl she is — really I'm sorry to leave you so soon," — the subject was cut short by the reply, stern and true, "No Sir, I'd die first." We are informed that many on the frontiers have deserted the "sealed relation" and married half-breeds and Potawatamies, preferring such a life as that in the cabins of Nebraska to the ennui of the other.

Young men, too, feel insecure in proposing to embark in the matrimonial vessel. They must naturally feel envious, when the young women treat them with disdain by yielding to the advice of ambitious mothers, and attach their fortunes to the hem of a president or apostle, in order to obtain a celestial queenship among the dignitaries of the world to come.

Of all the children that have come under our observation, we must, in candor, say, that those of the Mormons are the most lawless and profane. Circumstances connected with travel, with occupations in a new home, and desultory life, may in part account for this: but when a people make pretensions to raising up a "holy generation" and are commanded to take wives for the purpose, we naturally look at the quality of the fruit produced by the doctrines;—and surely they would not complain of the Scripture rule, "by their fruits ye shall know them."

Additions from abroad, and conversion of adults, can never sustain such a society, if the youth and children do not imbibe the principles that form the community and give it life and vigor — it is the young who are to transmit and inculcate them, or else, being at variance with their feelings and enlightened reason, the character of that society must soon change. For what constitutes society? It has been said, men make the state — this is true when the idea comprehends the humanity of man, wife, and children. No enduring blessing was ever promised to a people, without their children being expressly mentioned as participants; and heavenly pictures of a flourishing commonwealth are united with the merry gambolings and cheerful sounds of the young playing in the streets of busy cities. Break up the harmony of thought and purpose between the parent and child; make a man's enemies of his own household every where, and what becomes of society? It is at the *home*, at the fireside, at the family altar, that the principles and dispositions are obtained that govern individuals; and as the prevailing tone of the families, so will be the neighborhood, the towns, the legislatures; so too will be the union principle that constitutes a peaceful, prosperous state.

The first form of government, arising out of man's necessities and wants, is seen in the family, and is the Patriarchal; its inception is intuitive.

Now, we find the Mormons start in theory, right on the principle of Government, as on that of Labor. In true theory, government rests on the Divine Will, and human minds must interpret that will, either by direct revelation, or by Reason, enlightened by experience. Expediency, or what promotes human happiness, is the rule, but never to infringe on Revelation. In other words, Justice between individuals and nations is the *object* of law — leaving each person all possible freedom to choose his occupation. Security of Rights is the true political enonomy; the natural desire of good stimulates man to work out wealth and prosperity.

Try, then, this people by their own rule. We find them claiming to act by Divine Will and in the Patriarchal form. Look at its development! The divine will is changed at once into a scheme of Human Will — and the latter is made the Lawgiver — the Judge — the Executor. If the Seer is the Voice of God, all is well — right. The world denies this however. And then it falls into an autocracy, despotism.

So long as the governed people *choose* to obey one man in all things, they are not slaves — they may be secure in "life, liberty, and the pursuit of happiness," in their own estimation. Practically thus far the Mormons are so; and as education is spreading right thoughts and will continue to do so, if let alone, among the masses of Yankees and Chartists, they will learn how and when to throw off the usurpations of a pretended Theocracy.

In the family, the fostering restraint of authority is necessary till a certain age, and then the young bird, full fledged, flies off in joyous freedom, to assume its natural responsibility. So of Colonies — and this one, in the Rocky Mountains, now asks the privileges of manhood from the parent States — that granted, and the vagaries of its youth on the science of government will be discarded in the schooling of experience.

THE BIBLE.

But the proselyting from other Christian sects will be sadly interfered with, and checked, when the Bible shall be published as altered by Joseph the Seer. To be sure, each sect that gives an interpretation of the scriptures different from the apostolic sense, has a new Bible; but they all keep the same words, and individual judgment is the standard that causes diversity, which is ever changing; and thus there is left open the opportunity for a catholic, that is, universal opinion. But the Bible, printed with the emendations which we before referred to, will no more be the Christian's book of the present churches, than the Alcoran of Mahomet, or the Zendivesta. Then there will be something tangible, showing the tendency of the doctrines, and a direct blow be aimed at the "faith once delivered to the Saints;" it will no longer be, in the minds of any, a transition and progression from one view to another, but necessitate an apostacy from one religion to a different creed, and to the worship of a different God.

These adult additions for bettering temporal condition, do not add to the strength of the theo-democratic principle of their government. This will merely give power to the selfish element, to what they already complain is so common, and numerously represented by the "Mormonish;" while, to carry out the proposed plan, there is required the most complete disinterestedness; all that sinking of self in the prosperity of the order, so conspicuous in the devoted, holy brotherhood of the Jesuits. Whole families emigrate from abroad on account of the desire of a son, a daughter, or one parent, who are converts — the *faith* of one or two, perhaps, making the *occasion,* not the *motive,* for the other members joining the society.

A fourth disturbing cause lies in the system of tithes. By this engine, immense sums are accumulated, and put at the disposal of the Presidency, and its corrupting influences of irresponsible expenditure will sooner or later be developed. It cannot be long before those restless, ambitious, and talented persons, who are denied the great privileges which untold treasures secure, will become dissatisfied at the sight of ease and luxury in the managers of what they may consider a *religious speculation;* and some may envy the harems of the shepherds of the flock, supported indirectly by the labors of the hirelings. The toiling laborer in the dusty field may raise the question of unequal burdens, as the princely carriage rolls past with the music-band in the train, which even now makes melody in the visiting processions and pleasure-rides in the mountains. The means for amusing the mind of the multitude, and distracting attention from its own increasing power, are daily becoming less; while on the other hand, the burdens grow more and more onerous, and are less voluntarily borne. The pressure for tithes from all parts is again vehemently made, and reminds of the times of Joseph, when engaged on the Nauvoo temple.

Nor is the harmony and union of the Presidency so strong that it could not be broken. What could happen to the first three, with the prophet at the head, can easily occur again. It requires no great shrewdness to perceive the growing affection manifested for different persons in that board of directors, and parties will carry the object of admiration with them. No open organizations are yet made in favor of the second in rank, who is reported to be the best business man in the valley, but it would require but little tyranny, and novelty of doctrine, preached by the Seer, to cause the cry of apostacy and ambition. Like Lucifer and Rigdon, he would be declared, by a numerous host, to have forfeited the high estate, and a vote of the chiefs of stakes, or expressed will of the majority of the people, would depose him. At present he is wary of giving revelations, rather hinting that something is soon to appear, of wonderful importance. He assures that Joseph the Seer has left more work carved out, than five years of faithful diligence will accomplish — and when they have fulfilled all the duties entailed, then they may ask for more light from the angels.

All these seeds of distrust, ambition, and discontent, are sown in a fruitful soil; and if they are left quietly to germinate by the powers at a distance, cannot fail to destroy that unity which renders the Mormon community so formidable to any that might seek to control it. That people may well be compared to the Puritans of New England, in its early settlement — they are as exclusive, as energetic, as enduring; have sustained persecutions more fiery — have toiled for rocks and snowy lands — contended with the red men, and subdued a desert for a residence. May no General Gage be directed to dragoon them into rebellion. On one area the theo-democratic government has yielded peaceful fruits, and been forgotten — on the other, like results, we hope, are to follow.

There appears to be a crisis in the relations of the Mormons to the government of the Union, and sober counsels are demanded, to prepare the way for a peaceable, honorable future. No reference to State pride, no thought of religious aberrations, can be safely consulted in the case: nothing counselled but generosity on the side of power, towards those who have achieved so much in fertilizing a barren region, and made "two spires of grass to grow where only one grew before"— nothing but indulgent charity should be exhibited to men who declare themselves ready to enter upon an honest warfare of reason, enlightened by revelation, to maintain, if found good, or abandon, if demonstrated erroneous, long cherished opinions — and forbearance may honorably be exercised, while they continue to carry out practically the principles of republican liberty and human freedom, in accordance with American genius, though the method be theoretically absurd; having good assurance that there are improving elements within, that will "leaven the whole lump." Such conservative views will produce harmonious action, and the STATE OF DESERÉT become a sound connecting link in the great empire chain, whose termini are riveted in the everlasting foundations of the turbulent Atlantic and calm Pacific; those station points, at which the ascending sun salutes, and, descending, bids a short farewell each day, lightly kissing the snow-capt brow of the lofty mountain peak, that looks so serenely down upon the vales, filled with the happy homes of peaceful industry.

CONCLUSION.

Let us not then be the advocates of Mormonism, and opposers of our own form of Christianity, by counselling persecution and foreign control. This system is not what it was in its first decade.

Once it was aggressive, now it is on the defensive — then it was violent, now it is politic. The thousand mile wall of space uninhabited, hems it in and renders it harmless. The industry of its supporters makes it useful to the country. They are more than an army against the Indians on the West. The weary traveller o the land of Ophir shares in their hospitality.

Mormonism could not exist as a concrete system among other sects. It must rule or it must die. A fair field to test its virtues and its faults is before us. Its votaries are now to ascertain its claims to truth by prophecy. If, in a few short years, they see the great city of New York, its people, its temples, and its wealth, go down into the opening earth, and the sea sing a requiem over the grave—if they see the Protestant world become only known in the records of the past—if a guard of angels in glittering armor descend and guide them back in military array across the desert plains—if they hear the groans of the Asiatic nations, dying in frantic battle, in myriads, on the plains of Palestine; then may they know that the testimony of Joseph was of "the spirit of prophecy."

This new creed arose out of the strife of conflicting human opinions, and is one of the great exponents of the age, in which individual mind is struggling to throw off the fetters of superstition — and in the rebound to unbridled private judgment here is added one more instance of exalted genius enlisted on the side of priestly tyranny, and sacrificed on the altar of ambition — carrying hecatombs to an "auto da fé." Its founder will survive in history. He is embalmed in the affectionate memory of thousands; and as time lends a halo of enchantment to encircle his name, hymns of praise and legends of his holy deeds will be sung, and cherished by those who believe that the prophet saint of earth is to reign a God over a brilliant world of his own creation, surrounded by happy queens and carolling children, through his own blessed eternity. When the "knowledge of the Lord covers the earth as the waters cover the sea," then will this new church, the handy-work of man, fade away and be forgotten. For its virtuous industry we praise, for its brotherly unity we admire — and for its induction into the one Catholic Church we offer our sincere prayers.

ADDENDA.

MORMON CHRONOLOGY.

1823.

Joseph Smith announces a visit from the angel Moroni, at Palmyra, New York.

1827.

Golden plates, eight inches by four, connected by rings and engraved with Egyptian letters, given to Joseph by the angel for translation.

1830.

Book of Mormon published — Church organized and settled at Kirtland, Ohio.

1831–2.

New Jerusalem selected in Jackson County, Missouri — and named Zion — Corner stone of a Temple laid.

1833–5.

A mob at Zion drive the Mormons to Clay County — Kirtland named Shinahar, and store-houses, temple, and tithes arranged — Mercantile house formed.

1836–7.

Mormons driven from Clay to Caldwell, Missouri—Found Fai West—Bank of Kirtland established.

1838–9.

Bank fails — Danite Society organized — Third persecution in Missouri, and the Mormons driven to Illinois.

1840–1.

Nauvoo City laid off on the Mississippi—State of Illinois grant extraordinary privileges — Hostile feelings from citizens and dissenters appear.

1842–3.

Temple begun at Nauvoo — Charge of "Spiritual wives" denied — Polygamy granted — Troubles with civil courts.

1844–5.

Joseph the prophet and his brother Hyrum, repair to Carthage on charge of treason — Are shot in jail by an infuriated mob — Brigham Young chosen Seer — Violence offered to Nauvoo people — Burnings at Green Plains.

1846.

Property sacrificed at Nauvoo — Mormons emigrate to the Missouri Bottom — Cultivate land twenty miles above Platte junction — Battalion of 520 men recruited for the Mexican War — Women do field-work — Great sickness in camp — Caves dug for winter shelter.

1847.

Great mortality and suffering — Indians molest the Mormons — 8th April: Seer and advance guard of 143 men depart for the mountains — Seeds and implements transported — 21st July: Advance at Salt Lake Valley, and 24th Presidency arrive — Ground consecrated for a city — Invalid company of the Mexican battalion arrive, and 4000 persons come in October.

1848.

January: Fort completed, of 7788 feet contour — Thirteen miles of fence, enclosing 6000 acres, made—June: Crickets cut down the plants, which are renewed four times in some cases — People starving, dig roots and eat old hides — Five mills put in operation — Seer returns with emigrants — Settlements extended — Temple at Nauvoo burnt.

1849.

Utah Valley occupied — Large crops raised — Constitution for a territorial government made — Withdrawn, and one for a State sent to Congress — Survey of the valley by Captain Stansbury and Mr. Gunnison, made by order of United States — Tuilla and San Pete valleys colonized — Missionaries sent to France, Denmark, Sweden, and Europe generally.

1850.

University of Deserét incorporated — Schools opened — Cities laid off in Ogden, San Pete, and Timpanagos districts; and little Salt Lake Valley colonized — Iron mines worked — State-house finished — Governor dissolves the State provisional government, and the Territory of Utah recognised — Brigham Young appointed governor by the President — Tithing store-houses built, and adobes made for private dwellings — General prosperity.

1851.

Census taken — United States judges arrive — Become dissatisfied, and withdraw — Legislature protests — Sixteen mills in operation — Polygamy openly discussed — Latter-Day Saints ordered to remove from the frontier to Utah the coming year.

Photo of the Gunnison Monument, Massacre Site West of Hinchley, circa 1927.
From the archives of the Utah Historical Society.

The Gunnison Massacre Memorial

The remote area where Gunnison and his comrades were murdered was marked only by the two graves which held the remains of all the dead except Captain Gunnison and William Potter, the Mormon guide. The site was first marked thirty-five years later, in 1888, by Mormon Church Historian Andrew Jenson, who was guided to the spot by persons who had helped to bury the dead. This first memorial was a large cedar post.

The site was marked again, thirty-four years later, in 1922, the seventieth year following the massacre. Once more Andrew Jenson performed this service. He was accompanied this time by 63 other persons. A few stones were taken from a nearby corral and piled around the stump of the cedar post.

Five years later, on June 3, 1927, 3,000 persons were present to witness the unveiling and dedication of the splendid monument shown in the illustration. A large slab of basalt, taken from a nearby ancient lava flow, was shaped and imbedded in concrete. To this was affixed a bronze plaque bearing the names of the dead.

Gunnison's biographer, Dr. Nolie Mumey, of Denver, Colorado, visited the area in 1953. With the help of local residents, Gunnison's grave in the Fillmore city cemetery was located and properly marked. Mumey also visited the massacre site. He found the monument, but the plaque was missing. Another plaque, installed by the Daughters of Utah Pioneers, was subsequently removed. Through the intervening years the basalt stone has been chipped and fractured to a fraction of its original size.

Utah officials and interested citizens, now aware of these conditions, would prefer to create new memorials to Captain Gunnison and his comrades in places of greater public access, such as roadside turnouts, accessible campsites, and in museums and information centers along the Expedition's route.

Persons interested in helping to create such memorials may send their contributions to the Great Basin Historical Society, P.O. Box 550, Delta, Utah 84624.

The Unsolicited Chronicler reveals and unravels the twisting and long-buried course of events, showing how the murder of the Gunnison survey party led inexorably to the infamous Massacre at Mountain Meadows, to the Utah Expedition, and to a generation of conflict between the Mormons and the United States Government.

The author persuasively argues that in fact the life and fate of Captain John W. Gunnison may have been of utmost significance to Mormon development between 1847 and 1859. His relations with the Mormons, his book describing their history and beliefs, the massacre of his party, and the sequels which this unprovoked slaughter produced, lie prominently within the mainstream of continuity in Utah Territorial history during this period of time.

Dr. Fielding began his 14 years of painstaking historical detective work on the Gunnison Massacre while working on the CBS film project, "The Mountain Meadows Massacre." Examining, often for the first time, all the extant primary documentation, exploring long forgotten sites and gathering evidence, he assembled Gunnision's story from its clues and fragments. The result is a powerful and profoundly moving interpretation of events that establishes the life and death of Captain John Williams Gunnison as seminal to the history of the American West.

". . . A gripping examination that raises new questions while reviewing old ones. . . The Gunnison massacre now assumes a new significance. . . By candidly exploring things like blood atonement and the defensive atmosphere cultivated by Mormon apocalyptic belief, the reader is led to see how conflicts were nearly inevitable. . . [The book is] compelling and conceptually persuasive. . . I am immensely impressed." — ***Carmon Hardy, Professor of History, California State University at Fullerton.***